Life before birth

Life before birth

*A search for consensus on abortion
and the treatment of infertility*

Kenneth Boyd, Brendan Callaghan SJ
and Edward Shotter

First published in Great Britain 1986
SPCK
Holy Trinity Church
Marylebone Road
London NW1 4DU

Thanks are due to The British Council of Churches for permission to quote
from *Public Statements on Moral Issues* by the BCC and RC Liaison
Committee, 1978.

British Library Cataloguing in Publication Data

Boyd, Kenneth M.
  Life before birth: A search for consensus on
  abortion and the treatment of
  infertility.
  1. Infertility—Moral and ethical
  aspects
  I. Title   II. Callaghan, Brendan
  III. Shotter, Edward
  179′.76   RC889

  ISBN 0–281–04247–0

Printed in Great Britain by
Bell and Bain Limited, Glasgow

In order to get anything right, we are obliged first to get a great many things wrong.

Lewis Thomas, The Youngest Science

Contents

Acknowledgements

In preparing this book the authors were especially indebted to the following individuals: Dr M. Brueton, Dr C. T. Currie, Dr W. Cutting, Mr C. R. Dinnis, Professor G. R. Dunstan, Miss D. Forman, Professor T. W. Glenister, Mr J. Gollock, Dr D. Haskard, Dr R. Higgs, Dr P. Holland, Dr P. Huntingford, Mr G. Johnson, The Very Revd W. B. Johnston, the Revd D. J. Kellas, Professor I. Kennedy, the Revd M. Lefebure OP, Mrs L. McDiarmid, Mrs M. S. Macmillan, the Revd J. Mahoney SJ, Miss T. Moncreiff, the Revd S. Pattison, Dame Cicely Saunders, Miss E. Scott, Mrs A. Thompson, and Dr C. West.

The authors are also especially indebted to the Trustees of the All Saints Educational Trust, without whose generous support their work would not have been possible. In addition, they wish to thank the Edinburgh University Staff Club, the CIBA Foundation and the King Edward's Hospital Fund for London, for providing facilities.

Introduction

About this book

This book is the result of a three-year study, undertaken to explore medico-moral questions of multidisciplinary and ecumenical interest. It is particularly concerned with the ethics of abortion and the treatment of infertility. Its discussion of these questions is addressed, in the words of the study's original protocol, 'primarily to church leaders and theological students, but also to members of the medical and allied professions, to those concerned with policy-making and legislation, and to a general audience'.

The book is in two parts, the first about abortion, the second about the treatment of infertility. Each part is divided into three chapters. The first chapter in each part (chapters 1 and 4) is entitled 'Public Statements': these chapters summarise what has been said, on the respective subject, in a variety of significant parliamentary, professional and church statements. The second chapter in each part (chapters 2 and 5) is entitled 'Discussion': these chapters are the records of a small multidisciplinary working group, invited to discuss informally, and against the background of its members' professional and personal experience, moral questions similar to those with which the public statements are concerned. The third chapter in each part (chapters 3 and 6) is entitled 'Comment': these chapters are our own theological and ethical reflections on aspects of the discussion chapters, in the light of the public statements and other sources.

The structure of the book is such that the chapters on 'Public Statements' may be read as an introduction to official thinking on the subjects concerned, and as a guide from which students may proceed to the original sources. The 'Discussion' chapters also may be read on their own. Although the opinions expressed in the discussion chapters are not claimed to be representative of any but the individual members of this particular working party, we, the authors, believe that many of the arguments and assertions advanced by these individuals are not unrepresentative of opinions which might be found in many other groups of professionals and laymen, if convened in a similar way. The 'Comment' chapters may be more difficult to read in isolation from those preceding them, since at several points they refer back to the public statements or the discussion. Our advice to readers, thus, is to read the chapters of the book, or at least to scan them, in sequence.

Origins

This book originated in its authors' interest in the possibility of consensus in the study and discussion of medical ethics. However, consensus is an elusive goal in medical ethics, not least in relation to the particular subjects with which this book is concerned. In the past, when medical ethics was discussed 'by consultants, with consultants and *in camera*' (as one consultant of the 1960s put it, declining to take part in public discussion), some measure of consensus may have been possible, at least within the medical profession. But medical consensus often has been tacit rather than explicit; and, even in the past, different doctors commonly made different moral choices on the basis of different ethical or religious views.

Today, consensus seems even more difficult to achieve. Scientific, technological and organisational developments in medicine raise moral questions which, by common consent, cannot be answered adequately within the terms of traditional or professional medical ethics. Increasingly, therefore, these questions have become matters of public debate. But public debate in a modern pluralistic society commonly does not lead to consensus. Indeed public debate about the particular questions discussed in this book often leads to moral conflict and the entrenchment of polarised positions. This book discusses such conflict with particular reference to religious views. But, for example, philosophical analysis (in which almost all moral positions are endlessly contestable) often brings consensus no nearer; and discussion of these questions in the political arena typically makes any common agreement even less likely.

Conflict rather than consensus thus seems to characterise much public debate about medical ethics today. This need not be considered an unmitigated evil. In a classic study of 'tragic choices' in resource allocation, Calabresi and Bobbitt conclude that 'a moral society must depend on moral conflict as the basis for determining morality'.[1] But as these writers also observe, it is necessary for moral conflict to be expressed in ways which preserve 'the moral foundations of social collaboration'.[2] The danger, in other words, is that moral conflict, when the sole basis for determining morality, may escalate into actual conflict, anarchy or totalitarianism, thereby destroying either life or fundamental values. Against these eventualities, the attempt to determine an appropriate morality requires not only the stimulus of moral conflict, but also the discernment and cultivation of both existing and emerging areas of moral consensus. Achieving consensus on moral questions is, of course, not necessarily the same thing as discovering the truth about them. On the other hand, a willingness to engage in rational public discussion of moral questions presumably implies that the possibility of reaching some common agreement on them is regarded as at least one significant criterion of the correctness of whatever is agreed.

The need to discern and cultivate moral consensus was one of the presuppositions prompting the study which led to this book. The book originated in our association with the Institute of Medical Ethics, a non-partisan organisation for the multi-disciplinary study of medico-moral questions. Through our involvement in the work of the Institute (and the student Medical Groups associated with it), we were well aware of the vital contribution made by moral conflict to informed professional and public debate about medical ethics. By the same token however, we were aware also that, in some circumstances, moral disagreements could be an expression not of conflict between basic values and principles, but of lack of information, understanding, or good will. Ignorance or prejudice, not to put too fine a point on it, seemed sometimes to be responsible for conflict on certain medico-moral matters.

Conflict of this latter kind, of course, may sometimes prove unresolvable. On the other hand, a retreat to entrenched moral positions may reflect a need for time to understand the nature of what may be genuinely new medico-moral questions. Particularly in areas of rapid biomedical or social change, the

fundamental values challenged or supported by new developments may not be apparent immediately. In this context, the
authors' experience of a non-partisan and multidisciplinary
approach to medical ethics has persuaded them that debate on
these questions should begin not from beliefs held, but from
medical facts, and that the participants should listen to one
another open-mindedly as well as critically. We have observed
that, in so far as this is done, those involved commonly become
better able to discern, and discriminate ·between, areas of
genuine moral conflict and areas of existing or emerging moral
consensus.

The origins of this book are not only in our association with
the Institute of Medical Ethics, but also in the fact that we are
members of three different Christian traditions – Reformed,
Roman Catholic and Anglican. As such, we do not wish to
underestimate the differences between these traditions, particularly in matters of Christian ethics or moral theology. But
here too we believe it important to distinguish between moral
conflicts of a fundamental kind and those which arise as a
consequence of lack of information, understanding or good will.
In this context, the common Christian conviction that God 'is to
be found in all his works as well as in his revealed Word'[3]
provides theological encouragement to the search for consensus,
since it suggests that the Creator has not left his creatures
without clues, or without some ability to discern how the moral
life should be lived and a moral society fostered. In any attempt
to interpret these clues, we believe, the differences between the
Christian traditions are less important than what they have in
common, namely the hope that 'the moral dilemmas and often
anguished choices facing humanity today are ... so many
challenges to "achieve the truth in love" (Eph. 4.15) by responding to God's creative call as found within each situation.'[4]

This book records one attempt to respond to such a challenge. It does this, not by claiming to have discovered or
achieved consensus, but rather by exploring some of the per-
spectives, arguments and modes of moral reasoning which
require to be taken into account on the way to any consensus.
The fact that institutions and individuals may express themselves
in a variety of different ways is among the considerations to be
taken into account. Some of the opinions recorded may, of

course, be dismissed by some readers as of historical interest only, as marginal to current ethical or policy-making debate, as idiosyncratic or even as ill-informed. However, we believe that very many of the institutional and individual views it records have to be taken seriously, if the possibilities of, and obstacles to, consensus in current medico-moral debate are to be fully appreciated.

The general plan of this book is then that each part begins by summarising significant aspects of what are for the most part clearly focused public statements. The discussion chapters diffuse and fragment this focus in ways which may not be unfamiliar to those with experience of spontaneous discussion among practitioners and laymen. In the belief that these different ways of talking about medico-moral questions are each of significance for any possibility of consensus in medical ethics, the chapters entitled 'Comment' seek to refocus the discussion of some issues raised. Any further judgement on the value of this procedure must now be left to the reader. But before turning to the chapters themselves, it may be helpful to make a few more detailed preliminary observations about their content and method.

Public statements

The public statements cited in chapters 1 and 4 come from a variety of sources and carry different kinds of authority. The statements under the heading 'Parliamentary', for example, range from those which have full legal authority (e.g. the Abortion Act 1967 and the Surrogacy Arrangements Act 1985), to those whose moral authority depends upon judgements about the reasonableness of their respective arguments (e.g. the Reports of the 1960 Feversham and 1984 Warnock Committees). Some statements of the latter kind (e.g. the 1972 Code of Practice recommended by the Peel Committee) have achieved a degree of customary if not legal authority, which is shared by some of the statements appearing under the heading 'Professional and Scientific' (e.g. the original 1982 policy statement by the Medical Research Council on IVF research). Other statements under this heading vary in authority: statements, for example, on advising minors about abortion and contraception, issued by the General Medical Council and the British Medical Association, clearly differ from one another by virtue of the fact that the GMC is a statutory body with disciplinary powers, while the BMA is a professional association. Statements by the Medical Research Council, on the other hand, vary between those which are advisory (e.g. the MRC's 1985 'Response to the Warnock Report') and those (e.g. the 1982 policy statement on IVF research) which carry the authority of the major relevant body (a government agency rather than a government department) funding the research of the workers to whom the statement is primarily directed.

Church statements cited in chapters 1 and 4 also vary in nature and in authority, both within and between the churches. The subject of *Public Statements on Moral Issues* is fully discussed in a 1978 report with that title,[5] prepared by the Liaison Committee of the British Council of Churches and the Roman Catholic Church in England and Wales. A brief summary here of that report's findings (in relation to the Church of England, the Free Churches and the Roman Catholic Church) may help to introduce the church statements in chapters 1 and 4 below.

In the *Church of England*, while moral teaching is an integral part of the ordinary ministry of bishops and parish clergy, central church bodies also occasionally produce statements in response to particular problems. The latter, commonly occasioned by or anticipating 'a particular moment in the development of policy, practice or law', and addressed to the public, 'do not claim universal applicability, nor are they framed as exhaustive moral treatises on the subject under consideration'.[6] The ethical method adopted in making these statements relates different relevant general moral truths to the particular situations and contexts concerned. In doing this, 'Anglican moral reasoning assumes both the legitimacy of the use of reason in interpreting Scripture and Tradition, and the need to take adequate account of the results of empirical investigation';[7] in the latter, it pays particular attention 'to the ethical judgements and practice of those professionally engaged with the matter under enquiry, and to the development of professional practice'.[8] The consequent statements represent 'not magisterial declarations totally confined to the terms of a moral tradition, but the product of grappling with new questions in the light of that tradition, and in the process developing it further'.[9] In practice, these statements are commonly prepared by working parties, 'convened by the archbishops, by the Board for Social Responsibility or by some other authority within the Church',[10] it being these authorities' decision whether or not to make its findings public. Publication does not necessarily imply approval by the authorities. Some statements are brought before the General Synod and resolutions relating to them may be passed: but while 'these resolutions may add a degree of authoritativeness to the statement, its conclusions are not regarded as therefore binding on the consciences of individual Anglicans'.[11]

Statements of the *Free Churches* made in response to particular problems are produced by methods not dissimilar to those in the Church of England. In these statements, particular emphasis is commonly laid on 'whatever is understood to be the teaching of the whole of Scripture', as 'bound to be formative of Free Church thought'.[12] Statements usually 'are expressed as an argument' relating to 'the Bible, the tradition of the Church' (both that of the particular Church concerned and Christianity in general), and 'contemporary experience and the necessary empirical evidence' – the last after seeking, 'for example, the professional help of doctors in cases of medical ethics'.[13] Statements on moral issues are normally prepared by Church Divisions or Boards concerned with social responsibility. If 'affirmed and approved' by the Assembly or Conference of the Church concerned, they 'express the teaching of the Church at that particular time'; and 'all members of the Church are expected to receive the statement with the seriousness it deserves' as such. On the other hand, since not even the Church 'has an infallible apprehension' of God's guidance, 'the individual freedom to dissent reasonably is respected. Freedom of conscience is recognised ... It is perfectly possible to be a member of the Church whilst dissenting from the particular moral statement'.[14] This freedom of conscience extends to the individual church member 'acting in a manner contrary to [the statement's] affirmations'. But this 'does not mean open permissiveness, for historically at least the Free Churches have "disciplined" their members for what is taken to be unchristian behaviour'.[15]

These comments on Free Church statements are in general applicable also to those of the *Church of Scotland*, although the latter's established position as a national church means that, like the Church of England, it has a particular responsibility to take account of views beyond those of its own formal membership.

In the *Roman Catholic Church*, official moral statements represent 'a comparatively rare and *ad hoc* response by an appropriate body within the Church to an issue which it considers has reached a critical stage sufficient to require the intervention of the Church's teaching authority (*Magisterium*)'.[16] Such statements may be of different types. 'Statements addressed to the whole Church, or to "all men of good will",' include those of ecumenical councils, papal encyclicals, the Vatican's Sacred Congregation for the Doctrine of the Faith, as well as of the Synod of Bishops. Other statements are issued by regional or national hierarchies, sometimes differing in the 'nuances' of their 'local pastoral application of the Church's moral teaching', or dealing with 'a range of local or national moral questions'.[17] Of 'more limited ... application' are 'the regular pastoral letters of diocesan bishops', but 'occasionally also a diocesan, national or regional request for clarification or adjudication by Rome on a local matter will evoke a reply which may be interpreted as applying universally or as reinforcing a previous general statement'.[18] Other statements again, of international or national commissions, may produce 'public consultative or discussion-promoting documents' which 'do not address themselves directly to matters which are considered settled within the moral teaching of the Roman Catholic Church, but are devoted to subjects which are regarded as open for debate or to the application of the Church's traditional teaching in new circumstances and situations'.[19]

The Roman Catholic Church claims greater authority for its magisterial statements than do the other churches for those of their Synods or Assemblies. This is because

> the R.C. Church claims authority to interpret divine Revelation, which in turn is considered to illuminate and enrich natural law. For this, the authority attaching to the Spirit-enlightened source of a magisterial statement, as Pope Paul VI observed (*Humanae Vitae* 28), is 'no less' a motive for acceptance than the arguments contained in the statement.[20]

Within this context, Roman Catholic statements 'argue their case by appealing strongly to Scripture, to patristic teaching, to previous authoritative magisterial statements, to the Church's tradition and to human reason'.[21] It is important to note that, while 'the main point of a statement' is often 'to ascribe serious objective moral wrongness to a particular action', nevertheless, 'this is expressed in the context of a more positive and general theological and philosophical treatment of the subject'. Thus

> In denouncing certain actions as objectively morally wrong, RC statements do not automatically condemn individuals who may perform such actions, and some recent statements have explicitly drawn attention to the fact that performance of objectively wrong actions may not always be subjectively culpable or sinful.[22]

It may be noted also that 'the critical reception given by many Catholics to some moral statements in recent years' (a possibility which 'has always been acknowledged within Catholic theology') has challenged the expectation that 'statements expounding moral teaching' with 'a ring of authority ... will not be questioned or debated within the Church, but simply applied'.[23]

A further point made by the Liaison Committee may be added here, not least since it reflects our experience. The Committee observes:

> All the BCC member churches and the Roman Catholic Church agree that Christian moral reflection must be based on Scripture, on the tradition of the Church, on the moral experience of individual believers, and on the results of relevant empirical enquiry – all worked upon by reason – even though different churches may give differing emphasis to each of these resources. The area of agreement about the method of moral theology is thus sufficiently large to make co-operation both possible and fruitful.[24]

The fact that such agreement already exists may be worth underlining, because this (together with the fact that all church statements do not have the same authority) is not always fully appreciated by the media.

Discussion chapters

The two chapters of this book entitled 'Discussion' are edited extracts from the records of a small working group which met in Scotland at a time when the ethical debate on *in vitro* fertilisation was being opened up to a wider public but before the Warnock Committee reported. The aim of convening the working group was to explore how doctors and others, speaking mainly for themselves and to one another, might reflect on what they saw as the moral implications of medical practice and of their personal convictions. One justification of this approach to the study of medical ethics was that it explored an area which seemed not only relatively inaccessible to sociological research, but also not too far removed from that in which practical judgements about medico-moral problems were daily arrived at, acted upon and criticised. Moreover, this approach had already been used, not unproductively,[25] in studies undertaken by the Edinburgh Medical Group involving small working groups of practitioners and laymen. In that context, some academic justification had been given to the approach by recalling that Socrates' method of moral inquiry was to ask critical questions of experts, and that Aristotle had argued that ethics should begin, not from abstract principles, but from the actual moral judgements of people with some experience of life. In the case of both founding fathers of moral philosophy, the aim had been to gain some general clarification of the moral issues in the hope of reaching some broad consensus for practical purposes.

With such considerations in mind, we invited twelve individuals to form a group 'to discuss examples of current medico-moral dilemmas, in order to explore the extent of convergence and divergence in ethical attitudes to the subjects discussed'. The group held seven meetings, three of which are reported on in the discussion chapters. Six of the group were medical; they comprised three consultants – a geriatrician, a paediatrician and a surgeon – together with a general practitioner, a senior registrar in obstetrics and gynaecology and a final-year medical student. The other members of the group were three clerical and three lay church-members. They comprised: from the Church of Scotland, a parish minister and a nurse; from the Roman Catholic Church, a chaplain and a school teacher; and from the

Scottish Episcopal Church, a further chaplain (identified in the text as 'the Anglican chaplain') and a radiographer. The religious views of the medical members were not identified in advance, but informed local soundings were taken before the individuals concerned were invited, in order to secure some balance of interests and views consonant with the aims of the study. We, the authors of the book (identified in the text as 'the Secretary', 'the Chairman' and 'the Anglican priest'), also took part in the group's discussions.

At each of its meetings the group received a verbatim transcript of the previous discussion. In receiving this, its members expressed the view that their opinions should not be represented as either definitive or even necessarily representative of medical or ecclesiastical opinion. They were simply, as one of their number put it, 'a group of doctors and others, brought in after work and seated down to discuss'. The group undertook neither an exhaustive review of the current literature in medical ethics, nor a detailed examination of many philosophical and theological arguments relevant to the topics it discussed. Such tasks, the group and the authors believed, were more appropriately undertaken by individual scholars or by more specialist working parties. Those involved in the group were simply individuals with some experience of medicine and of life who, as another of them put it, had 'sufficient diversity to disagree but sufficient in common to converse'. As the same member put it, they hoped only to provide 'a contributory discussion, which may not lead to conclusions, but may provide a summary of a complex debate for people who do not agree with either or any point of view'. This comment was made in response to the criticism of another member, that the group was largely professional and middle-class, and hence unrepresentative of society as a whole. That criticism is not denied here. But it is difficult to see what other form of inquiry might provide a more authentic expression of such everyday aspects of conflict and consensus about the moral issues discussed: the alternatives of social inquiry, with questions set or data interpreted by academics, or of popular debate, in which the majority may not be informed and characteristically remain silent, also have their shortcomings.

At the end of its meetings, the Scottish working group

generously agreed that the transcripts of its discussions might be read by a consultative group convened to advise the authors on how to relate the discussions to public statements on the same subjects. This group met in London on a number of occasions in 1983 and 1984. Its advice is most gratefully acknowledged, but the authors alone must bear responsibility for the final form, content and shortcomings of this book.

Part One
Abortion

1   Public statements

Parliamentary and medical

The 1967 Abortion Act

Among public statements with implications for the ethics of
medical practice, those of Parliament have unique significance.
The *Abortion Act 1967* was intended by Parliament 'to amend
and clarify the law relating to termination of pregnancy by
registered medical practitioners'.[1] Before 1967, the law of
England and Wales had been clearly stated in the *Offences
against the Person Act 1861* (Sections 58 and 59): abortion,
attempted or procured either by the mother or another person,
was a serious criminal offence. In 1929, however, the *Infant Life
(Preservation) Act*, introducing the new offence of child destruction (i.e. killing a foetus capable of being born alive), stated that
this offence would not be committed if the foetus was killed in
good faith in order to preserve the mother's life. The distinction,
thereby admitted, between criminal and therapeutic abortion,
was enlarged by the 1939 case of *R. v. Bourne*, in which it was
acknowledged that,

> if the doctor is of the opinion, on reasonable grounds and on
> adequate knowledge, that the probable consequences of the
> continuation of pregnancy would indeed make the woman a
> physical or mental wreck, then he operates, in that honest
> belief, for the purpose of saving the life of the mother.[2]

The *Bourne* judgement did not go to Appeal. Nor did it
recognise any justification for therapeutic abortion in terms of
the condition of the foetus as opposed to that of the mother. It
was widely claimed, however, that despite the relative liberty
extended to doctors by *Bourne*, large numbers of criminal 'back-
street' abortions continued to be performed with harmful or even
fatal consequences for the women involved. After much public
debate and a number of unsuccessful Bills, the 1967 Act was
designed to amend and clarify the law by stating *inter alia* that,

1. Subject to the provisions of this section, a person shall not be guilty of an offence under the law relating to abortion when a pregnancy is terminated by a registered medical practitioner if two registered medical practitioners are of the opinion, formed in good faith –
(a) that the continuance of the pregnancy would involve risk to the life of the pregnant woman, or of injury to the physical or mental health of the pregnant woman or any existing children of her family, greater than if the pregnancy was terminated; or
(b) that there is a substantial risk that if the child was born it would suffer from such physical or mental abnormalities as to be seriously handicapped.

2. In determining whether the continuance of a pregnancy would involve such risk of injury to health as is mentioned in paragraph (a) of subsection (1) of this section, account may be taken of the pregnant woman's actual or reasonably foreseeable environment.[3]

Proposed amendments

Since 1967, there have been several parliamentary attempts to amend the Abortion Act, notably in Private Members' Bills of 1975 and 1979. These Bills sought to qualify the references (in 1(a) above) to 'risk' and 'injury' with the words 'grave', 'serious', and 'substantial', and also to remove reference to the comparative risks of continuing and terminating a pregnancy. One reason for these restrictive proposals is suggested by a comment in the British Medical Association's *Handbook of Medical Ethics* which alludes to an interpretation of the Act which may be widely held. The *Handbook* notes: 'because risk of injury to the health of the woman is statistically smaller if pregnancy is terminated in the early months than if it is allowed to go to term, some people argue that abortion is justified if the woman requests it.'[4] While noting this interpretation, the BMA *Handbook* also observes that any woman requesting abortion needs a doctor to carry it out, and that the Abortion Act 'contains a "conscientious objection" clause by which the doctor can refuse to participate in treatment, though he has a duty to assist the patient to obtain alternative medical advice ... if she wants it'.[5] Attempts to strengthen this conscience clause (which defends other health workers as well as doctors) also have been made since 1967. The 1979 Bill, for example, proposed to omit the Act's proviso that, 'in any legal proceedings the burden of proof of conscientious objection shall rest on the person claiming to rely on it'.[6]

A further area in which changes have been proposed is that of the age of viability. The 1979 Bill, again, sought to amend the *Infant Life (Preservation) Act 1929* by reducing the age at which the foetus might be considered capable of being born alive from twenty-eight to twenty weeks and by extending the Act's provisions to Scotland. This proposal reflected medical advances which made the survival of earlier foetuses more likely, and although it was not enacted the BMA *Handbook* advises:

> The doctor should recommend or perform termination after 20 weeks only if he is convinced that the health of the woman is seriously threatened, or if there is good reason to believe that the child will be seriously handicapped. If the doctor is uncertain he should always consult other colleagues, follow his own conscience, and act in the best interests of his patient.[7]

The 1979 Bill's proposal to extend the provisions of the 1929 Act to Scotland reflected the fact that Scots Law does not limit the age at which pregnancy may be terminated legally. In Scots Law, which is not governed by either the 1929 Act or the *Offences Against the Person Act 1861,* there has been a traditional emphasis on the importance of intent, implying some recognition of the distinction between criminal abortion and therapeutic abortion carried out in good faith by a doctor in the interest of the life or health of the mother.[8]

Parliamentary proposals to amend the 1967 Act have also emphasised the importance of making adequate counselling available to all women seeking abortion. A Select Committee set up to review the 1975 Bill agreed that such counselling should be encouraged, as did the proposed provisions of the 1979 Bill. The importance of counselling was also emphasised by a committee (the Lane Committee) set up in 1971 by the Secretary of

State for Social Services to review the operation of the 1967 Act.[9]

The Declaration of Oslo

The modern medical profession's major public statements on the subject are the World Medical Association's *Declaration of Geneva* (1948 and 1968)[10] and *Declaration of Oslo* or *Statement on Therapeutic Abortion* (*1970*).[11] The Geneva Declaration is a restatement of the fourth-century-BC Hippocratic Oath, which interprets the Hippocratic promise 'I will not give a woman a pessary to produce abortion' as 'I will maintain the utmost respect for human life from the time of conception'.[12] The Oslo Declaration quotes this phrase as illustrative of the World Medical Association's belief that 'the first moral principle imposed on doctors is respect for human life'. But it also recognises the 'dilemma' created by 'circumstances which bring the vital interests of a mother into conflict with the vital interests of her unborn child'. In these circumstances, 'whether or not the pregnancy should be deliberately terminated' will reflect a 'diversity of attitudes towards the life of the unborn child'. This, the Declaration states, is 'a matter of individual conviction and conscience which must be respected. It is not the role of the medical profession to determine the attitudes and rules of any particular state or community in this matter.'

Nevertheless, the Declaration continues, 'it is our duty to attempt to ensure the protection of our patients and to safeguard the rights of the doctor within society'. To this end, therefore, it sets out three principles (relevant 'where the law allows therapeutic abortion to be performed, or legislation to that end is contemplated, and this is not against the policy of the National Medical Association, and where the legislature desires or will accept the guidance of the medical profession'). The three principles are:

1. Abortion should be performed only as a therapeutic measure.
2. A decision to terminate pregnancy should normally be approved in writing by at least two doctors chosen for their professional competence.
3. This procedure should be performed by a doctor competent to do so in premises approved by the appropriate authority.

The Declaration also states: 'If the doctor considers that his convictions do not allow him to advise or perform an abortion, he may withdraw while ensuring the continuity of [medical] care by a qualified colleague.'[13]

The Declaration of Oslo further qualifies its own application by stating that it is not to be regarded as binding on any member association unless it is adopted by that member association. In this respect the British Medical Association, in its *Handbook*, remarks that the general principles of the Oslo Declaration are 'broadly applicable to practice in the United Kingdom'.[14] (Two subsequent developments at the time of writing are that the BMA is no longer a member association and that the WMA (Venice, 1983) has altered the original Geneva phrase 'utmost respect for human life from the time of conception' to 'utmost respect for human life from its beginning'.[15]) The *Handbook*, in addition to the points noted above, also advises the doctor to 'be prepared to make arrangements for the patient to obtain a second opinion', should the patient's 'immediate wishes ... conflict with the doctor's judgement of her best long-term interests'.[16]

Minors and abortion

A further matter discussed in the BMA *Handbook* is the question of girls under the age of 16 requesting termination without their parents' knowledge. On this, the *Handbook* recognises the conflict between professional secrecy and the doctor's responsibility to the parents. This dilemma, it states,

> cannot be resolved by any rigid code of practice. The doctor should attempt to persuade the girl to allow him to inform her parents or guardian, but what he decides to do will depend upon his judgement of what is in the best interests of his patient.[17]

Similar advice was given by the General Medical Council in its publication of 1983 on *Professional Conflict and Discipline: Fitness To Practise*:

> When a minor requests treatment concerning a pregnancy or contraceptive advice, the doctor should particularly have in mind the need to avoid impairing parental responsibility or

family stability. The doctor should assess the patient's degree
of parental dependence and seek to persuade the patient to
involve the parents (or guardian or other person *in loco
parentis*) from the earliest stage of consultation. If the patient
refuses to allow a parent to be told, the doctor must observe
the rule of professional secrecy in his management of the
case.[18]

Following the Court of Appeal ruling in the December 1984
Gillick case, however, this paragraph was altered to read:

Where a child below the average age of 16 requests treatment
concerning a pregnancy or contraceptive advice, the doctor
must particularly have in mind the need to avoid impairing
parental responsibility or family stability. The doctor should
seek to persuade the patient to involve the parents (or
guardian or other person *in loco parentis*) from the earliest
stage of consultation. If the patient refuses to allow a parent's
consent to be sought, the doctor should withhold advice or
treatment except in an emergency or with the leave of a
competent court; but in any event he should observe the rules
of professional secrecy.[19]

Subsequently however, in October 1985, the House of Lords
ruled on the case of *Gillick* v. *West Norfolk and Wisbech Area
Health Authority and the Department of Health and Social
Security*. In his statement of the Lords' majority view, Lord
Fraser of Tullybelton said that

there might well be cases where the girl refused to tell the
parents herself or to permit the doctor to do so, and in such
cases the doctor would be justified in proceeding without the
parents' consent or even knowledge, provided he was satisfied
that
(1) the girl would although under 16 years understand his
advice;
(2) he could not persuade her to inform her parents or to
allow him to inform the parents that she was seeking contraceptive advice;
(3) she was very likely to have sexual intercourse with or
without contraceptive treatment;

(4) unless she received contraceptive advice or treatment her physical or mental health or both were likely to suffer; and
(5) her best interests required him to give her contraceptive advice, treatment or both without parental consent. (*Times* 'Law Report', 18 October 1985)

Nursing statements

Recent major declarations on ethics made by the nursing profession (the 'International Code of Nursing Ethics' of 1965, the 1976 Royal College of Nursing's 'Code of Professional Conduct', and the 1983 and 1984 'Code of Professional Conduct' of the United Kingdom Central Council for Nursing, Midwifery and Health Visiting) include no specific reference to abortion. The 1983 UKCC Code does state however that the nurse should 'make known to the appropriate authority any conscientious objection she holds which may be relevant to her professional practice'; and also that 'where, from a professional stance, a law is considered bad or inappropriate it should be challenged through the due processes of democracy'.[20]

The Churches

A common tradition

Recent public statements by the Churches in Britain on the subject of abortion have for the most part taken the form of contributions to a wider public debate, before 1967 concerned with proposals for legal reform, thereafter with reform's consequences, in particular the greatly increased number of therapeutic abortions. In making these statements, the Churches have spoken against the background of a common tradition which seeks, in the words of an influential Anglican report of 1965 (*Abortion: an Ethical Discussion*) 'to assert, as normative, the general inviolability of the foetus' and, 'to defend, as a first principle, its right to live and develop'.[21]

This common tradition has its roots in what the early Christian Church taught about abortion (the Bible, Exodus 21.22 apart, says nothing specifically on this subject) and also in Christian moral teaching generally. In a statement of 1980

(*Abortion and the Right to Live*), the Roman Catholic Archbishops in Great Britain refer to 'Christian social teaching' as 'an appeal to the consciences of the relatively well off and powerful to give practical recognition to the humanity and rights of the poor and weak'.[22] This interpretation of Christian ethics is widely shared by many contemporary non-Roman-Catholic Christians, and indeed others who might well agree, as a matter of fact, with the Catholic Archbishops' further statement that 'unborn children in Britain today are a legally disadvantaged class; they are weak; are a minority'.[23] In practice, however, the conclusions which the other Churches draw from this are not in all cases the same as those of the Catholic Archbishops.

Different interpretations

Differences between the Churches arise over the interpretation of their common tradition's view of the moral culpability of killing a foetus. In their 1980 statement, the Catholic Archbishops mention that while the Church has 'never wavered in its teaching that abortion, at whatever stage of pregnancy is seriously wrongful', nevertheless 'for many centuries ... ecclesiastical penalties and censures for causing an abortion early in pregnancy were often less severe than for those for abortion later in pregnancy'. The reason for this, the Archbishops explain, is that 'Christians like others took for granted scientific and philosophical theories which suggested that the newly-conceived human being did not become formed or ensouled until several weeks after conception'. Today, by contrast, 'the course of human development' is 'much better understood' by 'modern science';[24] and it is now clear that 'at the time of conception there comes into existence a new life'. This new life, with its unique 'genetic code', the Archbishops state, 'is the life not of a potential human being but of a human being with potential.'[25]

A different interpretation of the tradition was suggested by the Anglican Report of 1965, quoted above. This noted that Catholic moral teaching had not always regarded killing of the foetus before animation as murder; and it suggested that the more absolutist decrees of Roman canon law seemed to have proved acceptable 'only because a casuistry accompanies them to define the limits of what they prohibit'.[26] In the view of the Report's authors, the 'absolute principle' that the foetus was 'in all circumstances inviolable' was 'a novel departure' from the Christian moral and legal tradition.[27] Any attempt, moreover, to identify if and when the foetus was a human being or had a soul, the Report argues, would 'inevitably be influenced by the evaluative conclusions we want to come to'.[28]

Moral absolutes and agnosticism

The 1965 Anglican Report, while carrying 'no authority beyond that of the group'[29] which prepared it for the Church Assembly of the Church of England, was officially welcomed by that body in 1966. Referring to the Report in a 1979 debate of the Church's General Synod, Dr John Habgood (then Bishop of Durham) remarked that:

> the main point the report was concerned to make and the point which I believe the Church of England has been committed to since, is that here we are dealing with a grey area in which it is very clear that abortion is undesirable but we cannot take our stand on some moral absolute by saying that, from the moment of conception onwards, a fertilised ovum ought to have in some measure the rights of a human being.[30]

The Church of England's 'degree of agnosticism' (as Dr Habgood called it) on this question was shared by a Report of the Church of Scotland Social and Moral Welfare Board, the conclusions of which were accepted by the Church's 1966 General Assembly: 'Traditional attempts to determine some point during pregnancy at which "human life begins" are inconclusive and are now irrelevant,' the Report stated. But the Board, commending the 1965 Anglican Report, also argued that 'the inviolability of the foetus is one of the fundamentals and must be defended'.[31]

Act and risk

The Churches of England and Scotland, then, have differed from the Roman Catholic Church in their view of what the Catholic Archbishops call 'the fundamental significance of the time of conception'. This difference may not, however, be the crux of the divergence within the common tradition. The earlier (1974) *Declaration on Abortion*, issued in Rome by the Sacred Congregation for the Doctrine of the Faith, while taking into account the kind of arguments from 'modern science' used by the British Archbishops, points out that:

> it is not for the biological sciences to pass a definitive judgement in properly philosophical and moral questions such as that of the moment when the human person first exists or of the liceity [*sic*] of abortion. From the moral viewpoint, on the other hand, it is clear that, even if there be some doubt whether the entity conceived is already a human person, it is an objectively serious sin to expose oneself to the danger of committing murder: 'He who will be a human being is already a human being'.[32]

In other words, what the Declaration here focuses upon as of prime moral significance is the *act* of murder. 'You shall not kill' (Exodus 20.13) is God's commandment. Any act which even *risks* disobeying this is forbidden. 'Neither divine law nor human reason', the Declaration goes on to say, 'admit any right of directly killing an innocent person.'[33] From this way of putting things, the statements of the other Churches differ in two ways: first, over use of the word 'innocent'; secondly, over the moral focus.

Innocence

In the 1974 Roman Declaration, the word 'innocent' is used only in the context just quoted. The British Archbishops however use it more extensively, commenting, for example, that their defence of the unborn is 'consistent with the whole Christian teaching about the right of the innocent to live',[34] and going on to argue that the right of self-defence, in the case of abortion as in warfare, is 'limited; it never entitles us directly to kill the innocent'.[35] This comparison of abortion with warfare relates to an attempt by some nineteenth-century Roman Catholic theologians to defend therapeutic abortion at a time when it was becoming, medically, a safer procedure. Among the arguments advanced was that a foetus which threatened its mother's life (e.g. in an ectopic pregnancy) might be regarded, by analogy with warfare, as an unjust aggressor against whom it might be justifiable to use force sufficient to protect the mother's life. In an argument of this kind, the foetus might be regarded as not 'innocent' (i.e. in the original Latin sense – *non nocere*; not threatening harm). Such argumentation, however, was rejected by Rome as a false analogy, given its refusal to regard the foetus as other than innocent (i.e. as morally blameless and therefore absolutely protected).

When statements of the other Churches differ from this, it is in either ignoring the word 'innocent' altogether (as does the 1966 Church of Scotland Report) or explicitly rejecting it (as does the 1965 Anglican Report). What the Anglican Report specifically rejects is use of the word to justify preferring foetal life to maternal, when the two are in mortal conflict – the implication being 'that the child is morally "innocent" whereas the mother may be presumed at some time to have committed actual sin; therefore the "innocent" life should be preferred to the "guilty"'. This argument, the Anglican Report's authors state, not only 'rests on a theory of morality, desert and retribution which we would not wish to maintain', but also 'imparts to the word "innocent" a meaning which does not belong to it in this context'.[36] This particular difference between the statements of the Roman Catholic and other Churches, however, may not be of major significance, since in the cases of maternal-foetal conflict which the Archbishops, for example, go on to discuss, the term 'innocent' is used in a rhetorical rather than the strictly factual sense; moreover the conflict is treated in terms not of 'morality, desert and retribution' (as in the argument criticised by the Anglican report), but of a possible appeal to self-sacrificial maternal love.[37]

The moral focus: act and conflict

A more significant divergence arises over the moral focus. While Roman Catholic statements focus attention on the over-riding importance of avoiding the forbidden act of direct killing, statements of the other Churches broaden the focus in order to give greater moral weight to the intentions, circumstances and consequences involved not only in the forbidden act, but also in its avoidance. The 1965 Anglican Report, for example, while defending the presumptive right of the foetus 'to live and develop', was also prepared 'to lay the burden of proof to the contrary firmly on those who, in particular cases, would wish to extinguish that right on the ground that it was in conflict with another or others with a higher right to recognition'. Accepting the possibility that such a 'higher right' might exist, the Anglican Report argues, is a necessary aspect of remaining faithful to the common tradition:

> Only so, in fact, can we maintain the *intention* of the moral tradition, which is to uphold the value and importance of human life. For invariably in this discussion the question must arise, which life? And the absolutist adherence to refusal of abortion *in all circumstances* might well result, in some, in a frustration of that intention.[38]

That the rights of the foetus might conflict with others having *some* right to recognition is not denied by the Roman Catholic statements. 'What makes the problem such a troublesome one', the 1974 Roman Declaration states, 'is the fact that in some cases, perhaps even in very many, the decision not to have an abortion endangers other important goods which men are likewise to protect and which at times may even seem to take priority over all others'.[39] Nevertheless, the Declaration continues, 'We must assert without qualification that none of those reasons justifies disposing of the life of another human being, even at its earliest stages ... Human life is too basic a good to be compared with and offset by even the greatest disadvantages.'[40]

Justifying circumstances

Pursuing the same general argument, the British Archbishops accept that women have 'rights in respect of their own bodies', but point out that 'no rights are unlimited'[41] and that the unborn child has the right specifically 'not to be made the object of attack' by 'any procedure or technique ... adopted ... with the intention of preventing the continuation' of the child's development before birth. Any such attempt after conception, 'even if it is called by other names, such as "contraceptive" or "menstrual extraction" and so on', is 'in fact an abortifacient'.[42]

The Archbishops then go on to consider a series of circumstances in which 'the burden of proof' (as the Anglican Report calls it) in favour of abortion might appear increasingly weighty. At one end of the series are what the Archbishops believe to be 'the vast majority of abortions'[43] under the 1967 Act, which are 'offered as a solution to problems of inconvenience or embarrassment, or of some risk to the mental or physical well-being of the mother, or perhaps her other children'. In these cases, they argue, any moral arguments in favour of abortion could 'equally be used as arguments for infanticide':[44] 'the unborn child has a claim which cannot be outweighed by inconvenience and risks and a life which cannot fairly be sacrificed for reasons of health'.[45] In the more difficult case of potentially handicapped children, the argument that the unborn child would be 'better off dead' was 'equivalent to asserting the essential rightness of euthanasia': it was also 'profoundly at odds with ... caring work for handicapped children and adults' as well as with the experience of 'the inner richness of human existence' of 'many handicapped people themselves deeply opposed to abortion'.[46] In another difficult case, that of rape, the Archbishops state that a woman is 'certainly entitled to defend herself against the continuing effects of such an attack and to seek immediate medical assistance with a view to preventing conception'. However, if conception has taken place, 'the requirements of the moral law, transcending even the most understandable emotional reactions, are clear: the newly-conceived child cannot rightly be made to suffer the penalty of death for a man's violation of the woman'.[47]

Danger of maternal death

The most difficult cases, from the Archbishops' points of view, are those in which there is danger of death to the mother. Some such cases (as Pope Pius XII observed in 1951) need not involve 'a *direct* attack on human life'. There are times when, 'interference with the unborn child is in fact an unintended, though foreseen, side-effect of procedures necessary to save the mother from some underlying or supervening condition that threatens her life. For example, a treatment for cancer of the uterus can be justified even if it also causes a miscarriage.' Even in these cases, however, it remains the doctor's duty 'to try to sustain the pregnancy so long as there is any reasonable prospect of saving both' child and mother.[48]

Such cases, the Archbishops point out, differ from those 'in which the life of the mother could not be saved without a direct abortion'. But the latter, they believe, 'in contemporary medicine are certainly exceedingly rare or perhaps non-existent'. Should they occur, however, 'a sensitive and upright conscience must in these cases be guided by the fundamental principles which govern all these matters: innocent life is not to be directly attacked; the unborn child has an intrinsic right to life'.[49] 'In such a situation', the Archbishops add, 'the law of God which is also the law of reason, makes exceptionally high demands.' While not arguing that the law of the land should enforce these demands, the Archbishops point out that, as in warfare, the Church proclaims moral principles 'which can on occasion demand heroic self-sacrifice'.[50]

In these Roman Catholic statements then, the prohibition of direct killing, or even of the risk of direct killing, remains firmly at the centre of the Church's moral focus. The other Churches, as already noted, betray not only greater agnosticism about the status of the foetus, but also a greater willingness to focus on other moral considerations. The 1965 Anglican Report, for example, in seeking 'to maintain the *intention* of the moral tradition, which is to uphold the value and importance of human life', focuses attention not only on the foetus (which 'has a moral significance in so far as it is potentially a human life') but also on the 'mother's life or health' in cases where pregnancy constitutes a 'grave risk' to this.[51] The 1966 Church of Scotland Report shifts the focus even further, stating that while 'the right to life' of the foetus 'must be strongly defended ... we recognise that this general right is, in certain circumstances, in conflict with other rights. In the Reformed Church, the paramount concern has been for the mother.'[52]

The justification of necessity

Broadening the moral focus in this general way, the 1965

Anglican Report argues that such conflicts may be considered appropriately in terms of the common-law concept of necessity: 'strictly speaking' the Report notes,

> it is necessity alone which makes lawful any surgical operation by removing it from the category of mutilation. As conditions of 'necessity' it is required that the evil averted by the operation must be greater than the evil performed; and that no more evil may be done than is reasonably necessary to avert the greater evil. It would follow that the threat to the mother's life must be a serious one to outweigh in seriousness the interference with the pregnancy and the killing of the foetus.[53]

Going on to consider such a serious threat, the Anglican Report follows the 1939 *Bourne* judgement, that 'preserving the life of the woman' need not be rigidly construed as 'preserving the woman from death'. Thus, the Report argues, the justification of necessity can be extended 'to cover a real threat to the physical or mental health of the mother, that is to her psychophysical well-being'.[54] Safeguards against this extension being abused must ultimately rest 'on the integrity of the medical profession and on a standard of practice based squarely on the medical indications and the best discernible interest of the patient'.[55]

A sufficient category

The justification of necessity, the Anglican Report argues, is sufficient to cover all justifiable abortions. In the case of a potentially handicapped child or of one conceived after rape, 'the ground of the decision' should be 'the prognosis concerning the mother as affected by the pregnancy in question', which in turn should be seen 'as integrally connected with the life and well-being of her family'.[56] In reaching a decision, however, interprofessional consultation is required: the Anglican Report expresses the hope that such consultation 'could result also – if properly recorded – in a genuine moral tradition in medical practice',[57] which might 'help to create uniformity of practice throughout the country' and 'help also to avoid that disingenuity in law or medicine which any inadequate reform is almost certainly bound in practice to invite'.[58]

In welcoming the 1965 Report, the Church Assembly of the Church of England stated that it did so because the Report 'stresses the principle of life for mother and foetus and urges the Church to preserve and demonstrate a balance between compassion for the mother and a proper responsibility for the life of the unborn child'.[59] Addressing the Convocation of Canterbury soon afterwards, the Archbishop of Canterbury expressed the view that the authors of the Report had been 'both wise and right' to recommend that the various possible justifications of abortion should 'as far as possible be dealt with under the category of risk to the life or mental or physical health of the mother'.[60]

Similar conclusions were reached by the 1966 General Assembly of the Church of Scotland. The Assembly did not consider 'that the pregnant woman being either defective or under the age of sixteen are sufficient grounds, by themselves, for termination of the pregnancy'. Cases of this kind, 'the matter of possible deformity', and conception after rape could all be dealt with under the general rubric of whether 'a registered medical practitioner' was 'of the opinion formed in good faith' that 'the continuance of the pregnancy would involve serious risk to the life or grave injury to the health whether physical or mental of the pregnant woman whether before or after the birth of the child'.[61]

The 'environmental' clause

The Churches of England and Scotland, in the years immediately preceding the 1967 Abortion Act, were thus in agreement that termination of pregnancy could be justified solely on the grounds of 'grave' or 'serious' risk or injury to the woman's life or psycho-physical well-being. Since many factors had to be considered in the medical assessment of the risks or injuries involved, the Anglican Report, in proposals for a draft Bill, had included a clause to the effect that 'account may be taken of the pregnant woman's actual or reasonably foreseeable environment'.[62] When a similar clause appeared in what eventually became the 1967 Act, qualifying its statement of the comparative risks of continuing and terminating the pregnancy, the logic of the Anglican Report (it has been suggested by one of its authors[63]) was destroyed – a point perhaps not lost on the General Assembly of the Church of Scotland which in 1967 stated that this 'environmental' clause was 'both unnecessary and undesirable'.[64]

Reform, counselling and conscience

Since 1967, the Church of Scotland General Assembly and the Church of England General Synod have repeatedly expressed a degree of unease with the workings of the Abortion Act, particularly as the practical implications of the clause comparing risks became evident. Both bodies therefore expressed qualified approval of the 1975 and 1979 Parliamentary Bills and both have frequently emphasised the need for more adequate counselling of women seeking abortion. The Synod and the Assembly also have argued that the Act's 'conscience clause' should be strengthened or at least more strictly observed.[65]

In this they are in agreement with the Catholic Archbishops of Great Britain, whose statement of 1980 called for administrative and legislative remedies for a situation in which medical personnel opposed to abortion were 'in effect, being debarred, or at least seriously deterred from pursuing their chosen speciality, not only in obstetrics and gynaecology, but in other medical spheres closely related to the abortion procedure'.[66]

2 Discussion

Introduction

The previous chapter outlined some public statements on abortion. This chapter, by contrast, records a much more informal discussion of this subject, by the group of professionals and lay people, the composition and character of which were indicated above in the Introduction.

The group's discussion of abortion was introduced by the gynaecologist who began by outlining the provisions of the Abortion Act. 'Risk to the life of the pregnant woman', the gynaecologist said, might arise in cases, for example, of severe diabetes or coronary heart disease: such cases however were 'rare, and the moral decision easy'. Examples of risk that the child might be handicapped were rather less rare: in Scotland, during 1981, 1.6 per cent of abortions (145 in number) were registered on these grounds, whereas only 0.3 per cent (28) were registered because of risk to the life of the woman. Risk of handicap, which now came to light because of antenatal screening (for example in the case of Down's syndrome (mongolism) or spina bifida, or if the mother had contracted rubella (German measles) in pregnancy), also raised greater moral problems. Most women now had ultrasound scanning, which may detect other abnormalities such as hydrocephaly (an excess of cerebrospinal fluid causing pressure on the brain) for which corrective treatment is available. But other forms of screening, such as amniocentesis (testing by tapping foetal fluid), could at present be undertaken only at a fairly late stage in pregnancy when abortion may be the only subsequent 'treatment'.

Most abortions, however, were performed on the grounds of risk to the physical or mental health of the woman: these constituted 96.3 per cent (7,032) of those registered in Scotland in 1981. (Risk to the physical or mental health of existing children accounted for 1.8 per cent (166).) What were seen as relevant factors in these cases, the gynaecologist suggested, included 'low income, overcrowded housing, several previous children, alcohol or drug problems, schoolgirl or "immature" pregnancies, rape victims'. In considering whether or not to terminate a pregnancy, the two doctors involved had to take account of 'the feelings and wishes of the mother or parents of the "unwanted child", the relative risks to both mother and child of continuing or terminating the pregnancy, the circumstances and the gestational age, all with reference to the 1967 Abortion Act'. It was also the case that the decision could be 'affected by external factors, the numbers being performed varying in different geographical areas, depending on the availability of resources and the individual policy of consultants'. This last consideration raised the moral question of whether the decision should be left to the medical profession, since in many cases it was 'not a clear-cut medical problem'. In this respect abortions on the grounds of risk to the health of the mother were particularly difficult. Requests for termination, the gynaecologist stated, were

> made on many grounds to which the Act may not strictly apply, or which are at least discussable, since they probably could go to term and adoption without too great risk. Common causes are failures in contraception (failure of safe period or intra-uterine contraceptive device, forgetting to take the pill, intercurrent illness altering the pill's effect, women having stopped taking the pill because of age). In the case of a pregnant unmarried girl in her late teens or early twenties, in a stable relationship planning marriage, but not feeling financially or emotionally competent, should abortion be agreed to?

General practice and counselling

Further information about the practice of abortion was provided by the GP. In the GP's experience, most patients were referred for termination on 'purely social' grounds. The vast majority, the GP suggested, had 'no medical grounds, no worrying mental or financial problems: they are mostly girls who have been pretty inadequate in contraception'. When these patients presented early in pregnancy, say from eight to twelve

weeks, and if they were reasonably articulate, they were normally 'referred to sympathetic gynaecologists'. Social class, however, could make a difference: as the GP put it, 'the middle-class
person is more articulate and mobilises resources to get advice,
the poor don't. The rich discuss things, the poor do not.' As a
consequence, among patients living, say, on a council housing
estate, there were often 'later presentations ... and so all the
more need to get them to hospital quickly'. This contrasted with
the middle-class patient who, even if 'afraid of or avoiding their
own GP', might go to a charitable clinic and be referred to the
same 'sympathetic' gynaecologists.

In few cases, the GP thought, was there much follow-up or
counselling by the GP or the hospital. In his own practice, the
GP stated, 'If someone is highly ambivalent I may refer them to
the Family Planning Clinic, the Brook Clinic or the hospital
social worker.' But in general there was 'no counselling and
discussion for an average teenager getting an abortion'.

In response to a question from the parish minister, 'Do any
women indicate any moral, religious or Christian problems or
Church relationship? Have they discussed the situation with a
minister, priest or Christian friend?' the GP replied, 'All will
have discussed it with someone – a boyfriend, mother, girlfriend;
at least patients of families in the practice will have done.
Transient patients – maybe waitresses and so forth – may not
have.' In most cases, by the time patients reached their GP
'their minds are usually made up', and once they had arrived at
the gynaecologist 'they are already far down the road'.

'Traumatic' experiences and the need for counselling

The lack of counselling, as indicated by the GP, clearly dis-
turbed some lay members of the group. In reply to one, who
asked whether there ought not to be more counselling, the GP
stated, 'I doubt whether there should be. I don't see people
upset by terminations. People are more deeply upset when they
are bereaved.'

This view (which provoked the parish minister to comment
that 'the baby is always upset and has no counselling') was
partly endorsed by the gynaecologist when the school teacher at
a later point in the discussion referred to abortion as 'a traumatic

experience'. 'Is it', the Secretary asked, 'a traumatic experience for everyone?' The gynaecologist replied, 'I'm sure it isn't', and went on to say,

> Certainly, if you focus on the mother herself ... then most women who seek an abortion feel extremely relieved after it's all over. Some of those who have conflicts about it may feel it extremely traumatic, perhaps because they're forced into a situation by circumstances. Many women who have had six children and who are forced through financial and social circumstances into having an abortion will feel dreadful regrets. The young girl who's never experienced childbirth and producing a child will feel quite differently.

While taking the view that abortion might not be traumatic for everybody, both the GP and the gynaecologist emphasised that some cases were more complicated. In this connection the GP mentioned the difficulties of later terminations, at eighteen or more weeks following antenatal diagnosis at about sixteen weeks. In such cases, the gynaecologist stated, 'The parents should not be asked to decide, if they don't understand what is involved: there should be no diagnosis without realisation of the need for a post-diagnostic decision (i.e. about abortion) ... Much more counselling is needed on this.' This point was also made by the surgeon, who argued that, in the case of a potentially handicapped child,

> Parents need to be informed before unleashing terribly difficult babies of this sort on society ... Parents need to be told of the severe effects on physical and mental well-being, and that despite the advances in obstetrics, termination is needed. Parents need counselling so that they can make an informed choice; they need to be informed of the consequences of handicap to family and society.

A further example of the need for counselling was accepted by the gynaecologist in response to a lay member of the group who mentioned the case of a depressive middle-aged mother of five, whose pregnancy was terminated 'almost without consultation or support from the GP or gynaecologist' and without a psychiatrist being involved. This, the gynaecologist observed, was a good example of termination on genuine 'medical grounds': but, in the gynaecologist's opinion, it was possible that, despite this, guilt feelings had inhibited the doctors from giving support which was so obviously needed.

'Medical' and 'social' abortions

From this discussion, it seemed that the medical contributors saw the need for counselling primarily in terms of a working distinction between 'social' and 'medical' abortions. 'Medical' abortions were those characterised, for example, by an identifiable psychiatric or serious physical illness in the mother or by antenatal diagnosis of likely handicap in the child. In such cases, counselling was thought important. 'Social' abortions, by contrast, were spoken of mainly with reference either to mothers of several previous children living in difficult socio-economic circumstances, or to younger girls who had been 'inadequate in contraception'. The older mothers might well need counselling, particularly if they were 'ambivalent' about abortion. But although some of the younger girls might also be ambivalent and so need counselling before they got on the 'tram-lines' of termination procedures, the majority were spoken of as seeming to know what they wanted. Not all of the doctors in the group accepted this last point however: the paediatrician, for example, asked whether it was realistic, in the absence of formal counselling, to expect genuinely impartial advice from family and friends – or even from the doctors involved, whose task, after all, was 'to make the system work'.

A different aspect of the distinction between 'social' and 'medical' abortions, which seemed important to the GP and the surgeon, was that 'social' abortions were technically more simple. This view, which clearly identified 'social' with early abortions, was expressed by the GP: 'Early is simple: at six weeks termination is easy. It may be covered by the euphemism of menstrual regulation. Technical advances make things simpler.'

The point was taken up and developed by the surgeon:

In practice, there is now a threshold: you can refer to abortion as just an advanced form of contraception; if you miss a period and take two tablets it can be referred to as late menstruation. Essentially, any method of contraception is a matter of not wanting the foetus, so it comes down to the question of whether we want contraception. 'Social' abortions are advanced contraception.

This identification of abortion as 'just an advanced form of contraception' was questioned by the gynaecologist, however, who felt that 'there must be a difference' between the two. The Catholic chaplain also questioned this general line of reasoning, arguing that the recognition of a 'threshold' and the distinction between 'medical' and 'social' grounds were not simply technical questions within medicine, but much broader questions of social philosophy.

Technical and moral questions

The Catholic chaplain's point was made in the light of various remarks by the doctors who had spoken. The remarks just quoted, about the technical simplicity of early abortions, for example, had been made against the background of two earlier comments by the GP and gynaecologist respectively. In discussing early 'social' abortions, the GP had referred to a 1973 ruling of the US Supreme Court to the effect that (as the GP put it) 'up to fifteen weeks the child was an integral part of the mother'. While it might be 'delegating ethical responsibility to others', the GP remarked, 'I find this ruling helpful'.

A little later in the discussion the gynaecologist, referring to the time of gestation up to which terminations were performed, remarked that, within the legal constraints, 'the limit the individual gynaecologist is prepared to go to' was based on a 'gut criterion'. When the Catholic chaplain then asked the GP if the 'lower limit' of fifteen weeks was also based on a 'gut criterion', the GP replied in the terms, noted above, of 'early is simple'. But, asked the Catholic chaplain, 'Is this only a technical question? Is the foetus just an integral part of the mother?' To which the GP replied, 'Medically, it is, up to fifteen weeks.' This reply was supported by the surgeon's comments about early abortion being 'an advanced form of contraception', and by the gynaecologist (after, as has been noted, questioning that particular identification) remarking that, in the case of early abor-

tions, 'gynaecologists are basically technicians: we must accept
the woman's request, and discuss with the social worker if
necessary'.

This last remark, it was understood, had to be regarded as a
comment less on standard gynaecological practice, which varied
from place to place and also among individual gynaecologists,
than on the kind of pressures acting upon gynaecologists in
centres where the 1967 Act was liberally interpreted. The
surgeon, commenting on these pressures, remarked, 'I didn't
become a gynaecologist because you have to decide to do all or
none up to certain limits. If I had to make great "soul"
decisions in each case, I would have to give up within six
months.'

Against the background of these comments by the doctors,
the Catholic chaplain identified two moral issues which he
thought the discussion so far had overlooked. The first, raised
by the view of the doctor as technician, was that of social and
political philosophy. The second, raised by what the GP had
said about technical feasibility and the surgeon had said about a
'threshold', was that of the status of the foetus.

Social philosophy

The issue of social philosophy, the Catholic chaplain suggested,
involved two kinds of question: on the one hand, questions
about the criteria used by doctors in deciding whether or not to
accede to a request for abortion; on the other, questions about
whether the decision should be taken by the mother and/or the
doctors, or whether it should be 'that of society as a whole'. In
the Catholic chaplain's opinion the doctors in the group were
adopting a 'utilitarian' stance and not considering the philosophical alternatives. The surgeon, for example, had spoken
earlier of 'unleashing terribly difficult' handicapped babies 'on
society'. But 'by what standards' was this being judged and by
whom? In determining 'what is for the good of the community',
the Catholic chaplain believed, 'the decision should be that of
the community as a whole, properly informed. At the moment,
we are embedded in utilitarianism.'

In making this comment, the Catholic chaplain was not
without medical support: the paediatrician, for example, ques-

tion whether the medical profession was 'the right forum for debating decisions' about abortion, and asked: 'how do we take the debate back into the public arena?' The medical student also commented that such decisions 'should be by society's judgement'. Whether this judgement could be taken other than under strong utilitarian pressures seemed to the student more doubtful however. His recent elective in India 'made me ask how you reconcile the necessity for contraception there, with papal statements'. And the Anglican chaplain emphasised the role of utilitarian arguments even more strongly, suggesting that, 'whatever grounds [for abortion] are proposed, the ultimate grounds will always be social usefulness. The rest is a gloss on society, which goes its own sweet way.'

Nature, utilitarianism and Christian conviction

These two last comments seemed to support the Catholic chaplain's view that the discussion – and indeed, the practice of abortion – was 'embedded in utilitarianism'. Before turning to his view of the philosophical alternatives, however, two further medical contributions to the discussion are worth noting, since each hints at arguments for liberal abortion practice, which cannot be entirely subsumed either under the rubric of 'utilitarianism' or under the view of the doctor as technician. Both contributions are related to the importance of *intention* in the ethical equation. The first, although not developed as a philosophical argument, was concerned with what might be called the intention of 'nature' – or at least with how arguments involving 'nature' and the 'natural' are perceived by non-theologians. Providing, almost as an afterthought, an additional reason for his remark that abortion and contraception were each 'a matter of not wanting the foetus', the surgeon commented that, 'you also have to bear in mind the vast natural wastage in ejaculate'. (In relation to abortion, of course, this point might have been made more appropriately by referring to the high number of fertilised ova which do not implant or to the large proportion of spontaneous abortions or miscarriages.)

The second medical contribution worth noting here was made by the GP and concerned the intention not of nature, but of the doctor. Asked what factors were relevant to his decision when presented with requests for abortion, the GP replied,

> I try to be consistent. If abortion is available I think that giving the choice to the mother is for the increasing good of society and for the benefit of children. Every baby should be a wanted baby. Abortion is part of the spectrum of our society, enhancing society.

This line of argument was, in the Catholic chaplain's terms, clearly 'utilitarian'. It was perhaps significant that the GP – whose religious affiliation, if any, had not been previously ascertained – chose to complete this statement by saying, 'I am pro-abortion as a Christian.' In the GP's case then, it seemed as if the Christian critics of abortion practice had failed to get their theological point across.

Language, values and reasoning

It was this failure which the Catholic chaplain had to address in moving from criticism of 'utilitarianism' to a positive view of a philosophical alternative. He began this task by arguing that two different ways of talking about the foetus were possible, 'the language of consequences' and 'the language of rights'. The language of consequences was used when people talked, as the Abortion Act did, 'in terms of comparative risks to the foetus, the mother and others; and therefore, the techniques of termination, and therefore things like periodisation, the first, second and third trimesters, the early and late trimesters and so on'.

'All such talk' of consequences, the Catholic chaplain stated, 'leaves out any question of rights', but matters were complicated by the fact 'that rights are a matter of values', and that when people talk about the status of the foetus, 'values are often not clearly expressed but camouflaged. Thus people talk variously of "the foetus", a "foetal infant", "a potential person", "a person", or "an individual"; and perhaps there are other ways of talking about the same reality.' The important point here, the Catholic chaplain argued, was to understand 'that the choice of term is a matter not of mere fact or description, but a matter of decision and evaluation. To my mind there is no neutral use of language: there is either an explicit or a concealed judgement of value; and this is therefore a matter of decision.'

The crucial decision in the case of the foetus, the Catholic chaplain went on, was in the judgement given upon such questions as 'What is being human?' or 'Who qualifies for membership of the human race?' as well as the further questions of 'Who does the qualifying?' and 'Can human life be destroyed?' The answers given to such questions had 'indications beyond the foetus', particularly about whether dependency was judged as diminishing, or as part of human personhood: 'for if the foetus, which is entirely and extremely dependent, is a human being', with rights, then other dependent groups, such as the psychiatrically ill and the elderly, 'have rights accordingly'.

All of this, however, was a matter of decision, from which it followed that 'disputes cannot be resolved by appeal to facts alone and that the real conflict lies elsewhere at some other level'. A helpful account of what happened at that other level, the Catholic chaplain suggested, had been provided by Cardinal Newman when he distinguished between 'the original process of reasoning' and 'the process of investigating our reasoning'.

All men reason [wrote Newman], for to reason is nothing more than to gain truth from a former truth, without the intervention of sense, to which brutes are limited; but all men do not reflect truly and accurately, so as to do justice to their own meanings; but only in proportion to their abilities and attainments. In other words, all men have a reason, but not all men can give a reason. We may denote, then, these two exercises of mind as reasoning and arguing, or as conscious and unconscious reasoning, or as Implicit and Explicit Reason.[1]

In the light of this analysis, the Catholic chaplain suggested, 'the true area of conflict' in which answers were given to the question about who qualified for membership of the human race, was at the level of this 'implicit reason' – a term which perhaps corresponded to what Polanyi had more recently called 'tacit knowledge' or to what Oliver Wendell Holmes was describing in 1882 when he wrote, in *The Common Law*, that 'the very considerations which judges most rarely mention, and always with an apology, are the secret root from which the law draws all the juices of life'.

The Catholic chaplain's argument then was that how the

foetus was described – in the language of consequences or in the language of rights – was a matter of choice at the level of 'implicit' or 'instinctive' reason, 'prior to argument or proof'. It was a matter, he said, 'of something we might call a logic of the heart as well as a logic of reason'. This might seem 'light years away from matters of appalling social conditions and the real reasons in the real world that drive people to abortion'. Nevertheless, he believed, 'these ultimate matters of right and wrong will remain' and 'all social policies must in the end be motivated and conditioned by choices at this level'.

Values and experience

This analysis of language, values and reasoning, presented less an alternative to 'utilitarian' or consequentialist ways of arguing about abortion than a defence of the possibility of an alternative. It was left therefore to the other Roman Catholic contributor, a school teacher who was also a mother, to speak in more contemporary and experiential terms about what she believed were the rights of the foetus. She did this by considering two factors which she thought militated against respect for the rights of the foetus. The first concerned contemporary expectations about babies, the second, the experience of women in pregnancy.

Medical science, the school teacher said, 'has raised people's expectations, so that we almost expect by right to be delivered of a perfect baby'. While there was 'nothing wrong in hoping and praying for a perfect baby', she did not think that parents today were 'psychologically prepared for the fact that a child may be born that is not perfect by accepted standards'. This, she felt, was a peculiarly modern expectation, conditioned by the experience of being given guarantees that household and other goods would be 'delivered in perfect working order, or if not, you return them and you do so until you are satisfied'. Today, she suggested, 'many of us almost expect that guarantee from the hospital and its staff. With the developments in ante-natal screening and *in vitro* fertilisation, I think it's small wonder that people have become intoxicated with the apparent power we have to create life, to manipulate genes, to manipulate conditions and in the end to produce a perfect specimen.'

Such expectations, the school teacher stated, raised again the Catholic chaplain's question of 'what it means to be a human being, as distinguished from other animal life'. 'Does one', she asked, 'have to be intelligent, physically strong, mentally all there, sexually potent, to qualify for membership of the human race? Or does the human race include the weak and the frail, the old, the demented, the physically and mentally handicapped?' To answer these questions, the school teacher said, she would simply quote a recent homily by Pope John Paul II. Talking about the sick, elderly, handicapped and dying, the Pope had said, 'Without the presence of these people in your midst, you will be tempted to think of health, strength and power as the only important values to be pursued in life.'

If expectations of 'a perfect specimen' and such mistaken underlying values comprised one of the factors militating against the rights of the foetus, a second was the experiential difficulty of talking about 'a foetus, which is totally dependent on the mother for survival, as having any rights, at least any rights that are independent of her rights'. To illustrate this difficulty the school teacher spoke of how, in her own experience,

> the thing that amazed me on the birth of our first child was the sudden realisation that here was a separate person from me. So long as one was pregnant, one could be deluded into feeling that the baby was totally part of oneself, didn't have a separate life from one's own life. But it was at birth that one could view this person and recognise that it was a unique child, a separate being, with separate rights from one's own. This realisation bursts on you when the child is actually born.

This aspect of the mother's experience – that 'when women are pregnant, particularly with the first child', they 'don't always feel that there is a separate identity, a separate person within them' – was a possible reason, the teacher thought, why women contemplating abortion did not really take seriously the thought that they had 'to consider the life of another potential being'. At this stage, she suggested, 'one is preoccupied with one's own predicament and circumstances'. Nevertheless, she stated, 'for the first nine months of a human's life', when 'it is voiceless, totally dependent on the mother, it does have an independent potential right to life'.

Résumé and response

Discussion of current abortion practices had raised questions about what the Catholic chaplain described as the 'utilitarian' approach of the medical contributors. This approach, he argued, appeared to be objective, but in fact reflected concealed value-judgements. How people spoke and consequently acted with regard to abortion was a matter of choice and decision, ultimately guided by 'a logic of the heart'. This logic, the school teacher suggested, might conflict with many women's experience of pregnancy and also with the expectations of a consumer society: nevertheless it spoke imperatively for respect for the rights of the foetus and for the values inherent in respect for the rights of all dependent people.

Responding to these statements, other members of the group seemed anxious not to dispute the fundamental values which they saw the Catholic chaplain and the teacher as defending. The main area of dispute, rather, was concerned with what one member of the group called 'the fine print' of the Roman Catholic position, and particularly its insistence on a virtually unqualified right to life of the foetus from the moment of conception. This insistence was criticised, on the one hand, for its emphasis on conception as the moral 'dividing line' with significance for human status and, on the other, for what was seen as a deficient sense of proportion in its absolute nature.

Conception as the moral dividing line

Until the question was raised by other members of the group, neither the Catholic chaplain nor the school teacher had in fact expressed the Roman Catholic view in its most rigorous form. The school teacher, as already noted, had referred to an 'independent *potential* right to life', while the Catholic chaplain had not directly addressed the issue, confining himself to the more general question of how the language of foetal rights ultimately derived from implicit reasoning. Under questioning, however, the Catholic chaplain's defence of foetal rights *from the time of conception*, appeared to derive not simply from implicit, but also from explicit reasoning.

The role of explicit reasoning in the Catholic chaplain's

argument was illustrated when the Secretary questioned whether the true area of dispute really was at the level of basic values. Many people, he thought, 'would say that there is a difference between a developed foetus and a non-human life', but while some would put 'the crucial point at conception, or implantation possibly, others would say that you need multiple criteria to decide where the point should be'. In response to this suggestion, the Catholic chaplain restated his position, that it was

> not irrational to look beyond and outside reason for your ultimate criterion. So that, to be unfashionable, I suppose that in my particular judgement I would be guided in the end by something I would call faith, which I think is not irrational, but is perhaps supra-rational. At the same time, you have to talk rationally; and I just do not see where you can legitimately draw a dividing line, not neurologically, not genetically and not logically, between conception and any other point on the continuum.

Under further questioning the Catholic chaplain held to this view. Other members of the group were less certain that conception was the crucial moment either biologically or ethically. The gynaecologist, for example, accepted 'that obviously the foetus is a potential human being from the point of conception' and saw this as supporting those who argued 'that abortion is wrong, it's killing potential human beings'. On the other hand, the gynaecologist was willing to give more weight to what the school teacher had suggested that many women felt: the view that 'the foetus is not an independent person until it's born, and even then it's still very dependent on the mother', provided support, the gynaecologist thought, for those who argued, 'that the woman has a right to choose'.

While the gynaecologist saw no way of mediating between these 'extreme views', the paediatrician wondered whether there might not be a legitimate dividing line at a later point than conception. It was possible, he suggested,

> biologically to make a dividing point by saying that up to a certain stage a foetus is not independently viable, meaning that in no way can it live. Now, of course, science is intervening all the time and pushing back this frontier and one could argue that ultimately it's going to push it right

back so that perhaps a baby conceived in a test tube may in fact be nurtured right up; and so that argument, we might say, breaks down. But at this point in time, so far as we understand it, there is this sort of threshold before which virtually no foetus has ever lived independently; and some people would use that as a division.

The possibility of a dividing line drawn at viability, the paediatrician thought, did not 'really interfere with the argument' the Catholic chaplain was presenting; and when the Catholic chaplain asked, 'because that presupposes that independent viability is a definition of being human?' the paediatrician agreed. But the Catholic chaplain clearly was unhappy with this view, which according to his argument concealed a value judgement about the foetus under the guise of an apparently objective scientific description. On the other hand, it seemed to the Secretary that the Catholic chaplain's argument itself could be criticised for concealing value judgements under apparently objective scientific statements, at least insofar as the Catholic chaplain took his stand on conception as the crucial change in status. The difficulty with this, the Secretary thought, was that a crucial aspect of the Catholic chaplain's argument – identification of the point at which the foetus was regarded as a human being 'with strict implications of the way in which you act towards it' – rested on the single criterion of modern biological knowledge. This criterion differed not only from the older, medieval Catholic view, which put ensoulment at a later point, but also from what had been said about the subjective feelings of many women. The problem about using this 'single criterion' he thought, was that it was 'making a moral argument from a piece of biological knowledge, perhaps even an "ought" from an "is"'. In the opinion of the Secretary, the attempt to identify when human life began simply on this biological criterion, without taking into account 'subjective as well as the objective' attitudes toward the foetus, obscured the degree of consensus that he believed existed on the more fundamental issues which the Catholic chaplain had raised.

A sense of proportion

The Roman Catholic position was also criticised for what at

least two members of the group saw as its lack of a sense of proportion when viewed in both historical and contemporary perspective. These critics were less sanguine than the Secretary had been about the role of subjective feelings. The Anglican chaplain, for example, protested that,

> there seems to be an assumption that it's self-evident that people who walk around on two legs or even people who've been born are human beings, whereas the history of political society would seem to indicate that people like children and minors who weren't taking a useful economic part in society were regarded as non-beings. One may deplore this, but the fact is that in pre-Reformation times, this sort of contempt for people who were fully born, had all their faculties, everything together, who were under a certain age, were just non-people; and it seems to me an arbitrary sort of division where you decide humanity begins and ends.

Much the same thing, in the GP's view, was still true. It seemed to him that, 'we're more concerned with the people who died in the Penlee lifeboat disaster than the millions who are dying daily in Bangladesh. I think there has always been a gradation in the human sphere of interest, from our nearest and dearest to people we've never heard of.' And when the Catholic chaplain interjected that there surely was 'a strong difference between not caring about people and actually killing them', the GP responded. 'But we can kill by neglect, we can kill by not implementing the Brandt Report, we can kill by a hundred other ways.'

Summary and conclusion

From this discussion of abortion and foetal rights it seemed that the doctors who had spoken were prepared to accept that 'the language of rights' was, in principle, no less legitimate a way of talking about the foetus than 'the language of consequences'. At the same time, they seemed somewhat less than convinced of the practical relevance of such distinctions. While agreeing that abortion had to be practised within a law shaped by public debate between the users of these different languages, they seemed to see little hope of any agreement between what the gynaecologist called 'the two extremes'. Moreover, in everyday practice, the gynaecologist said, the individual circumstances of the women involved 'come in and cloud the whole thing', so that these personal factors 'perhaps are more important than the fundamental issues' which the Catholic chaplain had raised. But to say this, the Catholic chaplain protested, was to make an implied value judgement about the facts: focusing on the doctor's view of the needs of the individual woman, rather than on the rights of the foetus, was actually choosing a moral stance.

The Catholic chaplain's protest was not contradicted. But something of the way in which it may have been heard was reflected in an exchange between the Catholic chaplain and another medical member of the group. The latter tried to sum up the discussion by saying, 'I see a pre-Reformation "there are moral standards" point of view and a post-Reformation "there is a moral debate" point of view; and I'm not sure how you resolve that without a Reformation.'

When the Catholic chaplain then asked, 'You think they're incompatible? You can't have a debate without standards,' the doctor replied, 'I'm glad we're allowed to have a debate.'

Abortion and contraception

Contraception was not discussed by the group in any detail, but two contributions on the subject are worth mentioning here, since they raise questions respectively about medical and Roman Catholic attitudes. The first contribution was by a lay member of the group who suggested, during the discussion of counselling, that a reason for some requests for termination might be that earlier requests for contraceptive advice or for sterilisation were not made, or hindered, by the patient involved perceiving their GP as being 'judgemental', or having a 'judgemental façade'. This contribution suggested that the image presented to the group of GPs as liberal, and of gynaecologists as 'basically technologists' was not universally experienced.

The second contribution on the subject of contraception was by the school teacher who, speaking from a Catholic point of view, asked why women were now demanding a right to abortion. Presumably it was not because they wished abortion as 'a good thing' in itself. But perhaps it was a cry for 'an end to sexual exploitation', part of a wider campaign by women 'for more control of their own fertility' which had hitherto been controlled by male dominance. In this context, the school teacher suggested that 'the appeal of the Billings Ovulation Method of natural family planning is that it demands mutual respect, co-operation from both partners. It doesn't work unless you have both partners willing to go along with this method.' This method, the teacher added, had been reported as 'reasonably successful amongst very poor people in Kenya, just because it came naturally to the people there to live in rhythm with the natural cycles of the body. This wasn't some foreign, scientific, difficult-to-understand process: it was something they instinctively understood.'

Turning back to Britain, the school teacher asked why there were now 'so many unwanted pregnancies amongst young unmarried people' and 'particularly among young Catholic girls'? Was not the reason, she asked, that they were 'not being educated to understand their own bodies – being given the necessary knowledge about contraception, the pros and cons, where to go for advice? Instead of which perhaps they're just getting no education along these lines, not being allowed the choice to decide for themselves as responsible human beings.' In this connection, the school teacher thought, a further question which had to be asked, particularly by Roman Catholics, was whether 'contraception is to be preferred to abortion?' As she put it,

if they are so strongly against abortion in any form, is it right that they should place contraception on the same footing and regard it as evil as abortion? I would say that obviously abortion is a far greater problem; and perhaps if people have to choose, then people need to be educated in responsible contraception to prevent so many abortions happening.

3 Comment

To students of the voluminous contemporary literature on the ethics of abortion, the discussion recorded in the previous chapter may seem rather superficial: not only are some of its empirical, historical and philosophical generalisations questionable,[1] but some of the topics it touches on have been discussed more exhaustively elsewhere. This comment might be endorsed by practitioners and laymen whose moral views are at variance with those expressed in the discussion. Others, however, might consider that the discussion recorded above is much closer, than is the language of public statements and academic debate, to the common moral discourse of those regularly encountering the realities of abortion, whether as practitioners operating under the Abortion Act or as members of the public to whose opinion the Act's critics and defenders appeal. For this reason, they might argue, anyone concerned with the ethics of abortion today ought to listen just as attentively to this informal kind of discussion as to the more formal statements of public bodies and scholars.

Styles of moral argument

If this argument is accepted, it would seem that there exists, on the subject of abortion, considerable divergence not only among the arguments of public statements and of participants in the discussion recorded above, but also between the different styles of moral argument used, on the one hand in public statements and, on the other, by those whose daily work brings them into close contact with the subject matter of these public statements. Does this mean (as many suspect) that there is little or no common ground or possibility of consensus on this subject? To try to answer this question, it may be helpful to compare some significant remarks made in the discussion with relevant aspects of the public statements. Two particular remarks, which on the face of things seem to be at odds with the public statements, may serve this purpose. Both were made by the GP. The first, 'I think that giving the choice to the mother is for the increasing good of society and for the benefit of children', may seem difficult to reconcile with the statements of Parliament and the medical profession; the second, 'I am pro-abortion as a Christian', may seem almost impossible to reconcile with relevant Church statements.

Legal, moral and clinical judgements

An immediate problem about the first of the GP's remarks is that 'giving the choice to the mother' is precisely what the *Abortion Act 1967* does not do. In law, women have no right to choose that their pregnancies should be terminated. They have, of course, a legal right to refuse an abortion, as they have to refuse any other medical treatment to which they do not consent, since this would constitute an assault upon them. But the Act states that abortion is not an offence only if the decision that a doctor may perform it is taken by two doctors on certain grounds. These grounds are 'medical' not because they specify any particular condition of health or disease, but because their relevance to a particular case is to be determined by 'registered medical practitioners'. In law, therefore, it is clearly to the doctor and not to the woman that the choice is given.

In advocating 'giving the choice to the mother', however, the GP may be presumed to know these legal facts: indeed, without them, the doctor would not be in a position even to consider 'giving' the choice. The GP's remark thus has to be seen as expressing a *moral* rather than a *legal* judgement about the woman's entitlement to request an abortion. He is talking, that is, not about the uncontestable requirements of the law, but about questions which, precisely because they are moral, are also contestable. In other words, a significant feature of moral or ethical questions is that they cannot be settled by a simple appeal to the facts (including the fact of the law) but only by public moral debate.

But if the GP is making a moral rather than a legal judgement, may he still not be advocating what the law disallows? In practice, it might be argued, what the law requires is that the doctor should base his opinion not on *moral judgement* but on *clinical judgement*. In referring to 'registered medical practitioners', is not the law placing the burden of decision on the latter rather than the former, so that any appeal is not to judgements subject to the rules of public moral debate but to the judgements, *in camera*, of those privy to medical knowledge and expertise? In deciding to give the choice to the mother (this argument might continue) the doctor is substituting moral for clinical judgement, reducing his (legally indispensable) opinion to a mere blessing of the mother's choice, and effectively abdicating his responsibility under the law.

This argument seems a strong one. It would· be much stronger, however, if the law had been framed without reference to the comparative risks of continuance and termination of pregnancy, and without allowing account to 'be taken of the woman's actual or reasonably foreseeable environment'. These features of the law make a clear distinction between clinical and moral judgement difficult to maintain in practice, for the doctor's clinical judgement must take into account the mother's own evaluation of her continued pregnancy. Without this, it seems likely that any attempt to purify clinical judgement of the subjective dispositions of the mother would force doctors back on the statistical criterion mentioned in the BMA *Handbook*, that 'risk of injury to the health of the woman is statistically smaller if a pregnancy is terminated in the early months than if it is allowed to go to term'.[2] But the problem about this criterion (excluding at this point the question of duties towards or the rights of the foetus) is that it is difficult to see how any doctor employing it could justifiably refuse any woman's informed and consenting request for abortion in the early months, unless the doctor's special medical knowledge and expertise enabled him to identify some condition which, in a particular woman's case, made the termination of her pregnancy a greater risk, to her health or that of her existing children, than its continuance.

Emphasising the doctor's clinical judgement at the expense of his moral judgement thus seems to lay on the doctor the almost forensic onus of seeking justifiable reasons to refuse any abortion requested in the early months. Clinical judgement, properly concerned with individualised treatment in the context of a therapeutic relationship, is thus reduced to the sense in which 'clinical' implies cold and functional detachment, concerned more with diseases than persons. But, if this reduction is to be avoided, it is difficult to see any other way, under the Abortion Act, in which clinical judgement can be purified of moral and hence contestable elements. The point here is not that clinical judgement cannot avoid being 'moralistic', but rather that it cannot avoid fallibility concerning the broad range of possible consequences which the Abortion Act requires the doctor to consider. That the Abortion Act itself seems to envisage the doctor exercising moral judgement is presumably implied by its requirement that the relevant medical opinions should be 'formed in good faith'.

Giving choice to the mother

The Abortion Act seems then to require the doctor to exercise moral judgement as well as, or as part of, clinical judgement. But the question may still be asked whether this allows the doctor to do as the GP suggests and 'give the choice to the mother'. If this implies that the doctor abandons all moral responsibility for the opinion which the law requires him to form – if, for example, he adopts the statistical criterion but not its forensic onus, and his approval of the woman's choice is given automatically – it is difficult to see how this can be allowed under the law. On the other hand, the doctor, without abandoning responsibility, may quite properly be expected to consider, even as part of his clinical judgement, the rights, wrongs and possible consequences of the patient exercising her own moral choice in the matter; and, having considered this, there may well be a sense in which 'giving the choice to the mother' is not incompatible with the law. At the same time, the doctor should not be expected to abdicate his clinical expertise entirely in favour of the mother. He may, for instance, have good grounds (either in general or in this case) for judging her own prognosis of continued pregnancy unjustified or un-acceptable – in which case it would be difficult to consider his compliance with her request as made 'in good faith'.

In considering the moral and practical aspects of 'giving the choice to the mother', the doctor would seem to have at least two options, at least in the early months (and, for the present purpose, continuing to exclude the question of duties toward or the rights of the foetus). The first option might be for the doctor to judge that it was both right and wise to protect women from choice in the matter of abortion. The moral judgement here might rest on the principle of *beneficence*, interpreted as the doctor's duty to care for and act in the best interests of those in a vulnerable position. In practical terms, the doctor might argue that he was protecting the patient from the risk of making a choice (to have an abortion) which might subsequently be regretted, causing guilt feelings and possible harm to her health.

The second option, by contrast, might be for the doctor to judge it both beneficial and right for women to make their own choice in the matter. In practice, it might be argued, while it is a proper exercise of medical beneficence to take decisions on behalf of highly dependent and vulnerable patients, it is not appropriate to do this in the case of a conscious competent adult. To do so might be more harmful than beneficial to a woman's health, increasing the dependency of some and the desperation of others. It would also conflict with the view, widely held in other areas of medicine, that it is generally beneficial for patients to participate in choices affecting their own health. Such practical considerations might not be sufficient, of themselves, to determine whether a particular woman's health was likely to be harmed by denying her the liberty to make her own choice. But the principle of *respect for persons* might also be invoked here, and this principle involves respect for the individual's moral autonomy. Acting in ways which facilitate the patient's exercise of that autonomy thus could be justified on this ground as well as that of a proper beneficence.

Taking this second option then, it could be argued, a doctor would not be abandoning his legal responsibility if he regularly 'gave the choice to the mother', and as regularly approved that choice. To remain within the law, however, the doctor would have to satisfy himself 'in good faith' that his clinical judgement, here as elsewhere, was properly concerned with individualised treatment in the context of a therapeutic relationship. A general rule of 'giving the choice to the mother' would thus in principle always have to allow for exceptions, even if it is difficult to see what, in practice, would count as a justifiable exception in the case of a doctor who had adopted the rule and was asked by a fully informed and competent adult to terminate her pregnancy.

The GP's advocacy of 'giving the choice to the mother' would not then seem entirely incompatible with the terms of the Abortion Act. Nor would it seem incompatible with recent statements of the medical profession which retreat, or advance, so far from the Hippocratic prohibition of abortion as to consider 'therapeutic' abortion at least as a matter 'of individual conviction and conscience',[3] and which sum up the profession's duty in this area as 'to attempt to ensure the protection of our patients and to safeguard the rights of the doctor within society'. The crucial ambiguity about this statement is related to the question so far excluded from these comments – that of whether or not the foetus also is the doctor's patient.

Utilitarianism

Before turning to this question, a final comment may be made about the GP's first remark. A possible moral justification, suggested above, for 'giving the choice to the mother' depends on accepting the fundamental principle of respect for persons. This justification is not necessarily implied in the GP's remark, which argued that 'giving the choice to the mother is for the increasing good of society and for the benefit of children. Every baby should be a wanted baby. Abortion is part of the spectrum of society, enhancing society.' In the group's discussion, this kind of argument was criticised as 'utilitarian', the implication being that such arguments tended to promote 'mere utility', or perhaps simply convenience, at the expense of more fundamental rights and duties. But this popular use of the term 'utilitarian' may obscure the fact that arguments based on the concept of utility or 'the greater happiness of the greatest number' are not necessarily in conflict with arguments based on rights, duties or respect for persons. Some forms of utilitarianism, it is true, have crudely equated happiness with pleasure or have subordinated individual rights to the common good. But some more recent forms of utilitarian argument take the view that happiness is best defined by the individuals concerned and that respect for the rights, persons and choices of individuals is desirable for the common good.

It would be over-ambitious of this comment to read too many philosophical refinements into the GP's remarks. Nevertheless a remark such as 'every baby should be a wanted baby', although often used as a slogan, does rest in some measure on the idea of respect for persons, and cannot be dismissed simply as an argument from 'mere utility'. On the other hand, had the GP rooted his argument more firmly in the principle of respect for persons, his position might have been less contestable. As it stands, it is vulnerable in the way in which utilitarian and consequentialist arguments generally are vulnerable: that is, whether the particular good consequences the GP saw as flowing from abortion really are good, may ultimately be very difficult to establish, as may the credentials of anyone who claims to be a judge in the matter. That the GP did not rest his argument on respect for persons may be seen as reflecting the constraints of the Abortion Act upon his style of argument. But it would be unfortunate if such legal constraints obscured the moral issues involved, particularly since the variety of moral arguments implied in the GP's remarks suggest that further exploration might lead to greater consensus than appears either in the discussion or among some of the public statements.

Christians and abortion

This possibility of greater consensus, however, is suggested in the context of a discussion of abortion which has so far excluded the question of duties towards or the right of the foetus. Turning to the GP's second remark, 'I am pro-abortion as a Christian', this question becomes harder to avoid, since all of the Churches, whatever qualifications they may subsequently make, begin from the common tradition which seeks, 'to assert, as normative, the general inviolability of the foetus'. From such common ground, the most which might be asserted is that some abortions might be a necessary evil. But the GP seems to be suggesting that abortion generally is a positive good. On the face of things, his remark seems completely incompatible with the statements of the Churches. However, rather than simply leaving it at that, it may be useful to look briefly at the range of options open to someone in the GP's position who, as a Christian, might wish to justify abortion.

Clearly, the least likely place to find any such option is in the statements of the Roman Catholic Church. That Church's opposition to direct abortion is unqualified. Questions may be raised (and will be discussed later in connection with *in vitro* fertilisation) about whether killing an embryo before implantation actually is abortion, since it may be argued that the correct definition of abortion is the ejection of an immature foetus from the *womb*. But the public statements of the Roman Catholic Church leave no room for doubt that direct killing of any embryo after the moment of fertilisation is forbidden. What the British Catholic Archbishops state about a woman's entitlement, after rape, 'to seek immediate medical assistance with a view to preventing conception'[4] does, at first sight, seem to leave a loophole not found in their Church's general prohibition of artificial contraception. But even in the extreme circumstances of rape, medical intervention of this kind is permitted only if conception has not yet occurred. In this situation, the doctor following Catholic teaching would have the responsibility for conscientious professional interpretation of the facts: he would, in other words, have to decide within a very short time whether it was possible that conception had not yet occurred, and that he might thus intervene to prevent it. But the doctor's room for manoeuvre within the constraints of the Church's teaching here would be very small indeed.

Double effect

The only other possible exception to the Roman Catholic Church's prohibition of abortion concerns a very limited number of cases, mostly confined to removal of a cancerous uterus or an ectopic pregnancy. In Catholic thinking, however, these are not strictly exceptions, since they are not examples of direct killing. As Pope Pius XII put it:

If, for instance, the safety of the life of the mother-to-be, independently of her pregnant condition, should urgently require a surgical operation or other therapeutic treatment, which would have as a side-effect, in no way willed or intended yet inevitable, the death of the foetus, then such an act could not any longer be called a *direct* attack on innocent life. With these conditions, the operation, like other similar medical interventions, can be allowable, always assuming that a good of great worth, such as life, is at stake, and that it is not possible to delay until after the baby is born or to make use of some other effective remedy.[5]

This application of what is called the principle of *double effect* also leaves very little room for manoeuvre to the doctor conscientiously attempting to follow Roman Catholic teaching. The principle recognises that the doctor's act may have two effects, first the saving of the mother's life, and second the death of the foetus. But it insists that the second must not be willed or intended, even if it is inevitable. Moreover, the purpose of the act (the first effect) must represent an important good in itself (saving the mother's life) which is not achievable by any less extreme means and which will counterbalance the harmful effect to the foetus. It might be argued that the principle of double effect could be extended to cover other effects which are good in themselves, such as that of preserving the physical or mental health of the mother. And Pope Pius XII does refer to 'a good of great worth, such as life'. It is, however, central to Roman Catholic understanding of the principle of double effect that the act which leads to both good and bad effects should itself be morally blameless (such as removal of a cancerous uterus or a pathological fallopian tube); for otherwise it would be seen as a case of making the end justify the means.

Conscience and reason

In Roman Catholic teaching, then, there are no loopholes or exceptions by means of which a direct abortion, after conception, is permissible. There is thus no way in which the GP's remark could be made by a doctor conscientiously seeking to follow that Church's specific teaching on the subject. On the other hand, it is not impossible that a Roman Catholic doctor might seek to justify direct abortion under certain circumstances by appealing to his Church's teaching on the subject of conscience. He might point out, for example, that the Church's public statements on abortion do not claim to be infallible; and he might also point out that the Church teaches, in the words of the Second Vatican Council that, man perceives and acknowledges the imperatives of the Divine law through the mediation of conscience. In all this activity a man is bound to follow his conscience faithfully, in order that he may come to God, for whom he was created. It follows that he is not forced to act in a manner contrary to his conscience. Nor, on the other hand, is he to be restrained from acting in accordance with his conscience, especially in matters religious.[6]

With these considerations in mind, the doctor might argue, there could be circumstances in which he is not personally obliged to follow the Church's teaching, even in the face of highly authoritative pronouncements. Such circumstances might arise when the Church's statement of 'the law of God which is also the law of reason'[7] (as the British Catholic Archbishops put it) seemed to the doctor, in all conscience, not to be reasonable. Of course, to claim this responsibility of conscientious dissent from Church teaching lays considerable weight on the doctor's good faith, particularly since he is dissenting from teaching so unequivocally stated by the Church. Moreover, it is difficult to see how the doctor could appeal to the law of reason in making any claim that direct killing of the foetus was in itself a positive good, since in the Western tradition the normal philosophical as well as theological presumption would be that killing (even of non-human life) rather than not killing has to be justified. The most, perhaps, that the doctor might argue was either that certain cases of foeticide did not amount to homicide, or that foeticide might be justified, in certain cases, on the ground of necessity, or of the need to choose the lesser of two evils.

Necessity and dissent

The possibility that certain cases of foeticide do not amount to homicide will be commented on later, in connection with the subject of *in vitro* fertilisation. At this point, however, it may be recollected that the Anglican and Reformed traditions are much more agnostic than the Roman Catholic about the extent to which the fertilised ovum, from the moment of conception, ought to be accorded the full rights of a human being, and hence whether foeticide, particularly in the early months of pregnancy, amounts to homicide. But even in the case of foeticide the Churches of England and Scotland lay the burden of proof on those who seek to justify extinguishing the foetus' moral right to life on the ground that it is 'in conflict with another or others with a higher claim to recognition'.[8] And the only justification which these Churches are prepared to accept for this is that of necessity, which (in the words of the 1965 Anglican Report) requires that 'the evil averted by the operation must be greater than the evil performed; and that no more evil may be done than is reasonably necessary to avert the greater evil'.[9]

On these grounds also it is difficult to see how the GP can consistently claim to be 'pro-abortion as a Christian', if this remark implies that abortion is a positive good. The most that could be argued in accordance with the public statements of these Churches is that in certain cases abortion might be justified as a necessary evil, but only if the evil averted involved 'grave' or 'serious' risk to the particular mother's life or psycho-physical well-being. The GP's remark, however, seems to go beyond this, and to claim that the evil averted by abortion is *generally* greater than the evil performed by it, and that this evil generally cannot be avoided by any less drastic means than abortion. To make this claim 'as a Christian', the GP thus would have to claim, like the theoretical Catholic doctor discussed above, some responsibility for conscientious dissent from stated Church teaching. In the Anglican and Reformed traditions such a claim would probably be less controversial than in the Roman Catholic: but a doctor holding this view 'as a Christian' equally would be expected to be prepared to defend it according to the rules of rational public argument. How this might be done, in terms of respect for the mother's moral autonomy, has been suggested earlier. But a consistent argument would also require the doctor to express an opinion on the degree of the evil performed by abortion in relation to the question of the moral rights of the foetus. In the discussion, the GP remarked that he relied for this purpose on a 1973 ruling of the US Supreme Court to the effect that 'up to fifteen weeks the child was an integral part of the mother'.[10] It seemed to be the GP's conscientious view that up to this point foeticide need not be considered as homicide, thus limiting the degree of evil performed. Taking these various considerations into account, it would not seem to be inconsistent for the GP to say that as a Christian, conscientiously dissenting from the stated teaching of the Anglican and Reformed traditions on some matters but not others, he was not opposed to abortion, up to fifteen weeks, as in general a necessary evil. Such a restatement of the GP's position is not suggested here primarily in the interest of theological purism. Rather it is a matter of protecting the degree of moral consensus which still exists in society, against the rhetoric of moral polarisation.

Part Two
The treatment of
infertility

Introductory note

In Britain today, it is commonly estimated, around 10 per cent of couples are childless. It is not known, however, how many of these couples are childless by choice and how many are infertile. Among the latter, the causes of infertility may lie in either or both parents and can be relatively simple or very difficult to investigate. Where the cause can be identifed, treatment may take the form of medical or surgical intervention to assist conception following normal sexual intercourse. Much of the ethical and legal debate in this area, however, has been concerned with techniques which do not involve normal sexual intercourse.

The technique of artificial insemination (AI) with either the husband's semen (AIH) or that of a donor (AID) has been used with increasing success for several decades. AI involves obtaining semen by masturbation and injecting it into the neck of the woman's womb, the latter being a relatively simple procedure. AIH is essentially a matter of building up the semen and helping it on its way. It may also be used, if the semen is preserved by freezing, after a husband's vasectomy or indeed after his death. AID, by contrast, is employed when a husband's semen is seriously defective, either in terms of fertility or genetically.

The much more recent and complicated technique of *in vitro* fertilisation (IVF) is primarily concerned with female infertility. In IVF, an egg is removed by a minor surgical procedure from a woman's body and then fertilised with semen in the laboratory (*in vitro* literally means 'in glass', i.e. in the laboratory dish, hence the popular term 'test-tube babies'). The fertilised egg, now termed an embryo, is then implanted in the womb either of the woman from whom the egg was taken (this is termed embryo replacement) or of another woman (this is termed embryo transfer). The semen used, as in AI, may be that either of the woman's husband or of another male donor. The donor of the egg or of the semen (the sexual reproductive cells are known collectively as gametes) and the recipient of the embryo differ in different cases depending upon which individual is infertile and for what reason. A further technical possibility is that of fertilising eggs *in vitro* which are intended not for replacement or transfer but for the purposes of scientific research, not exclusively related to infertility.

4 Public statements

Parliamentary

The Feversham Committee (*1960*)

Major parliamentary statements on AI and IVF were made in
1960 and 1984 respectively. In 1958, public concern about the
growing practice of AID had led to the creation of a Departmental Committee on Artificial Human Insemination, chaired
by Lord Feversham. Reporting two years later,[1] the Feversham
Committee dealt both with the practice of AI and with its legal
consequences for the child thereby conceived. The Committee
judged that AIH was an acceptable form of treatment when
medically indicated. But, believing that it reflected both public
and medical opinion, the Committee expressed strong disapproval of AID and sought to discourage it. The Committee was not
prepared to make AID a criminal offence however. On the
question of legal status of the child, the Committee was in no
doubt (although some of its members regretted the fact) that the
child conceived by AID was illegitimate. Couples who, in
registering the birth, stated that the husband was the father,
were thus committing an offence.

Despite the Feversham Committee's disapproval, the practice
of AID continued to grow. In 1968 the Government agreed that
both AIH and AID, when medically indicated, might be made
available within the National Health Service. It was subsequently proposed (by a British Medical Association panel in
1973) that NHS centres offering AID should be accredited. This
was not implemented, and as a consequence it has proved
difficult to estimate the number of births following AID,
particularly since it seems probable that many such births,
despite Feversham's warning, may have been illegally registered
as legitimate. The Royal College of Obstetricians and Gynaecologists has suggested that in 1982, for example, there were 'over
1,000 pregnancies conceived and at least 780 live births following AID'.[2] But the Warnock Committee considered this 'un-

doubtedly an underestimate';[3] and another authoritative source suggested that AID 'gives rise to between 2,000 and 4,000 live births a year in the United Kingdom.'[4]

The Warnock Committee (1984)

By the end of 1984 the number of babies born in Great Britain as a result, not of AID, but of IVF was over 200. This was about a third of the world total, and included the first, born in Oldham in 1978. The rapid pace of development in this field led, in 1982, to the establishment of a Departmental Committee of Inquiry into Human Fertilisation and Embryology, which was chaired by Dame Mary Warnock and reported in 1984. Also among the reasons for undertaking this Inquiry was the concern that AID had been 'left in a legal vacuum'.[5]

Infertility treatment in general

The recommendations of the Warnock Committee presupposed a general view of infertility treatment. This rejected the argument that such treatment was either 'unnatural' or inappropriate to an over-populated world.[6] Moreover, infertility came within modern medicine's proper concern with 'remedying the malfunctions of the human body' and hence was 'a condition meriting treatment',[7] for which provision should be made, and monitored, within NHS priorities. Not everyone seeking such treatment might be eligible (the Committee expressed doubts, for example, about single parents or lesbian couples, believing that 'as a general rule it is better for children to be born into a two-parent family, with both father and mother').[8] But if a consultant declined to provide treatment, the patient should be given 'a full explanation of the reasons'.[9] Three general principles applicable to all 'techniques for the alleviation of infertility' were those of anonymity, counselling and consent: donors and recipients should not know each other's identity; counselling should be routinely available to all parties; and the written informed consent of couples should be obtained before treatment.[10]

AIH

On the subject of artificial insemination, the Warnock

Committee's views were more favourable than those of the Feversham Committee fourteen years earlier. Warnock recognised the sincerity of those who argued that AIH unnaturally separated 'the unitive and procreative aspects of sexual intercourse', or who had moral objections to masturbation. But this did not reflect the majority of views expressed to the Committee, nor its own view, which was that there was 'no moral objection' to AIH.[11] (The Committee did believe however that 'the use by a widow of her dead husband's semen for AIH ... should be actively discouraged'. To this end it recommended legislation to disregard, in matters of succession and inheritance, 'any child born by AIH who was not *in utero* at the date of death of its father'.[12])

AID

Considering arguments against AID, the Warnock Committee noted that the law did not equate AID with adultery and that AID lacked the personal relationship involved in adultery.[13] The husband's consent to AID, moreover, suggested 'a mark of stability in a marriage'.[14] The donor, as a third party, the Committee believed, did not necessarily threaten the exclusive marital relationship. Harmful tensions might subsequently build up between the couple, or the child might be harmed if he accidentally discovered his origins: but the kind of problems involved existed and often had been overcome in the analogous experiences of step-parenthood and adoption. The risk of a donor passing on a harmful genetic condition could be minimised by limiting the number of donations from any one donor.[15] Against all these objections (as well as against fears about the imponderable consequences of AID for the family and society generally), the Committee believed, there had to be set the fact that AID was a simple, painless and 'not particularly invasive' way of helping a couple to have a 'very much wanted child' whom they could 'bring up as their own' and who was 'biologically the wife's'.[16] A further, no less important consideration, the Committee added, was that 'the practice of AID will continue to grow, with or without official sanction and its clandestine practice could be very harmful'.[17]

In order to minimise the risks of AID and to regularise the

legal position of the AID child, the Warnock Committee made a number of specific recommendations. Semen donors should not be paid and they should be limited ('since some limit should be imposed') to fathering ten children.[18] Donors should have no parental rights or duties in respect of the AID child who, in turn, would be treated as the legitimate child of the infertile couple; the child could be registered as that of the husband, whose consent to AID would be assumed unless the contrary could be proved. While the anonymity of donors should be preserved, 'basic information about the donor's ethnic origin and genetic health' (to be held in a central register) should be available to the couple and, at the age of eighteen, to the child.[19]

Egg and embryo donation; surrogacy

Principles similar to those underlying the Warnock Committee's recommendations on AID informed its recommendations on human egg and embryo donation: a limited number of donations, anonymity but with access to genetic information, and clarification of parental rights and duties.[20] In these cases, the woman giving birth was to be regarded as the legal mother of the child.[21] Consistent with this recognition of the carrying mother's rights and duties, and also with the principle that donors should not be paid, were recommendations (from which two members of the Committee dissented) making criminally liable professionals and others, but particularly commercial agencies, who assisted in establishing a surrogate pregnancy (i.e. one in which the carrying mother, after giving birth, handed over the child to a commissioning couple – either or both of whom might or might not be the genetic parents).[22] Pending more comprehensive legislation on the Warnock Committee's recommendations, the Government-sponsored *Surrogacy Arrangements Act 1985* made illegal both commercial surrogacy arrangements and advertising in relation to surrogacy.

IVF

The Warnock Committee argued that its acceptance of egg and embryo donation was logically consistent with its acceptance of

AID and IVF. Discussing the latter, the Committee believed
that some objections (e.g. that it separated the unitive and
procreative) were substantially the same as those against AID
and could not be relied upon 'for the formulation of public
policy'.[23] Others, objecting to this use of expensive resources,
constituted 'an argument for controlled development, not an
argument against the technique itself'.[24] More serious, however,
was the objection (related to the clinical desirability, in current
IVF practice, of producing more embryos than would eventually
be transferred to the mother's womb) that it was 'not acceptable
deliberately to produce embryos which have potential for human
life when that potential will never be realised'.[25] This objection
was supported, in an Expression of Dissent, by three members
of the Committee.[26] While noting this objection, the majority
believed that IVF was 'an acceptable means of treating infertility' which 'should continue to be available within the NHS
although initially on a limited basis with its progress being
carefully monitored'.[27]

Licensing and research

One of the Warnock Committee's main recommendations was
the creation of a new statutory licensing authority 'with substantial lay representation' to regulate all infertility services and
research both within and outside the NHS.[28] Among the matters
for this body to consider would be 'the need for follow-up
studies of children born as a result of the new techniques'.[29] A
further responsibility of the licensing authority would be to
promulgate 'guidance on what types of research, apart from
those precluded by law, would be unlikely to be considered
ethically acceptable in any circumstances and therefore would
not be licensed'.[30] The Warnock Committee's own recommendations about what should be 'precluded by law' were chiefly
concerned with research on human embryos created by *in vitro*
fertilisation. Such research should be allowed only up to fourteen days after fertilisation, after which it would become a
criminal offence.[31]

This limitation derived from the principle, agreed to by the
whole Committee, that 'the embryo of the human species should
be afforded some protection in law'.[32] The particular limit of

fourteen days derived from scientific recognition of this as the latest time at which twinning and certain other variations could occur, and in that sense as marking 'the beginning of individual development in the embryo'.[33] The majority of the Committee agreed to set the limit at this point because, however arbitrary any point chosen might be, 'some precise decision must be taken, in order to allay public anxiety'.[34] Three members of the Committee (whose reservations about IVF are noted above) dissented from this, arguing that no experiments on the human embryo should be permitted.[35] A further four of the Committee's sixteen members, while willing to permit research on embryos created but not used for implantation in a mother, were not willing to agree with the majority that it should also be permissible to undertake research 'on embryos brought into existence specifically for that purpose or coming into existence as a result of other research'.[36] Among the Committee's unanimous recommendations about research were provisions to restrict to the two-cell stage of development trans-species fertilisation (for therapeutic or diagnostic ends) involving human sperm or eggs, and to prohibit the placing of a human embryo in the womb of another species.[37]

Other recommendations

The Warnock Committee's remaining recommendations covered a variety of technical questions related to research and to inheritance law. There were also a number of proposals for setting five or ten-year limits to the storage of frozen semen and embryos.[38] The Committee saw 'no objection in principle to the use of freezing in the treatment of infertility', but recommended that freezing should not be used if an 'unacceptable risk' was involved (which there still seemed to be in the freezing of eggs, but not of semen and probably not of embryos).[39] One important legal recommendation was that there should be 'no rights of ownership in a human embryo', but only a 'right of use or disposal': this should be vested initially in the couple who stored the embryo, but on their death or disappearance, or if they disagreed about its fate, the right would 'pass to the storage authority'.[40]

The Peel Committee (*1972*)

The Warnock Committee's terms of reference, concerned with the six weeks immediately following fertilisation, precluded it from considering legal and ethical questions about foetuses of greater gestational age, which might become available for research purposes following termination of pregnancy. A Code of Practice to regulate 'The Use of Fetuses and Fetal Material for Research' had already been recommended in the 1972 Report of a DHSS Advisory Group chaired by Sir John Peel.[41] In the view of the Warnock Committee this Code, while not legally binding, had 'worked well'. But since Warnock was now proposing 'stringent legislative controls on the use of very early embryos for research' it seemed only logical that the research use 'of whole live aborted embryos or fetuses' should also be brought within 'the sort of legislative framework proposed' in its own Report.[42] In its 1985 Reponse to the Warnock Report, however, the Medical Research Council argued that 'the use of fetal material obtained during termination of pregnancy ... and related matters should be clearly excluded from any legislation'. In the MRC's view, the voluntary Peel Code worked 'effectively'.[43]

Dead foetuses, foetal tissue and foetal material

The Peel Committee's recommendations were made on the understanding that, 'in general', the contribution of research on foetuses and foetal material 'to the health and welfare of the entire population' was 'of such importance that the development of research of this kind should continue subject to adequate and clearly defined safeguards'.[44] In this context, it was permissible to use the whole dead foetus, foetal tissue (parts or organs of the foetus which might continue alive for a period after the whole foetus has died) and foetal material (the placenta and other contents of the womb apart from the foetus). In the case of the dead foetus or foetal tissue, use would be subject to the provisions of the Anatomy Acts 1838 and 1871, and to the absence of any 'known objections on the part of the parent who has had an opportunity to declare any wishes about the disposal of the fetus'. It was stipulated, further, that there should be 'no monetary exchange for fetuses or fetal material'.[45]

Live foetuses: viable and before delivery

In the cases of foetuses remaining alive after separation from the mother, the Peel Committee distinguished between viable and pre-viable foetuses. In the light of modern medical techniques the Committee considered that a period of 20-weeks gestation (corresponding to a weight of 400–500 grammes) should be regarded, subject to review, 'as *prima facie* proof of viability'. Where a foetus was viable after delivery, it was 'unethical to carry out any experiment on it' which was 'inconsistent with treatment necessary to promote its life'. Similarly, the only investigations or tests permissible on the foetus prior to delivery were those 'carried out with the intention of benefiting the mother, her expected child, or both'. The intention of terminating a pregnancy provided no ethical or legal justification for carrying out 'any procedures on the mother with the deliberate intent of ascertaining the harm that these might do to the fetus'.[46]

Live foetuses: pre-viable

Research on the pre-viable foetus, the Peel Committee explained, took the form of 'observations ... necessarily limited to a period of two or three hours'. Such research had 'already contributed significantly to our understanding of vital physiological and biochemical processes before birth on which the development of a fetus into a normal child essentially depends'. It might thus 'ultimately benefit viable infants'. Considering whether such research was ethically justifiable, the Committee 'noted that society through Parliament, in permitting abortion in certain circumstances has accepted that when an abortion under the Act is carried out the pre-viable fetus is prevented from attaining life'. It also noted that 'in the pre-viable fetus of 300 grammes or less as distinct from the fetus approaching full term those parts of the brain on which consciousness depends are, as yet, very poorly developed structurally and show no signs of electrical activity'.

The Committee thus agreed that pre-viable foetuses weighing less than 300 grammes might be used for research, subject to the conditions it had specified for the use of dead foetuses. In each case, the Committee stated, the responsibility for deciding that the foetus was in the permitted category should rest 'with the medical attendants at its birth and never with the intending research worker'. Moreover, the research might be carried out only in hospital departments and with ethical committee approval: the ethical committee would have to be satisfied not only of the validity of the research and the investigators' facilities and skill, but also 'that the required information cannot be obtained in any other way'.[47]

Professional and scientific: IVF

Before the publication of the Warnock Report, and independently of it, a number of professional and scientific bodies had made statements on ethical issues related to human fertilisation and embryology. Notable among these were statements by the Medical Research Council (1982),[48] the British Medical Association (1983),[49] the Royal College of Obstetricians and Gynaecologists (1983),[50] and a Working Party of the Council for Science and Society (1984).[51] Other statements, in the form of submissions to the Warnock Committee, or of responses to its Report, were made by a large number of scientific and professional bodies. These included, for example, the Royal Society (1983),[52] the Royal College of General Practitioners (1983)[53] and the Medical Research Council (1985).[54]

Medical Research Council (1982): IVF research

The earliest statement on human IVF research, that of the MRC in 1982, stated that 'scientifically sound research' in this area should be allowed to proceed on certain conditions. These included local ethical committee approval and the informed consent of sperm and ovum donors, including donors of embryos fertilised but no longer needed for therapeutic purposes. The aim of the research should be 'clearly defined and directly relevant to clinical problems such as contraception or the differential diagnosis and treatment of infertility and inherited diseases'. There should be 'no intent to transfer to the uterus any embryo resulting from or used in such experiments': nor should such embryos 'be cultured *in vitro* beyond the implantation stage' or 'stored for unspecified research use'. Research on the freezing and storage of embryos should be undertaken first on animal models. Non-human ova fertilised with human sperm (to provide information 'on the penetration capacity and chromosomal complement of sperm from subfertile males') 'should not be allowed to develop beyond the early cleavage stage'.[55]

British Medical Association, Royal College of Obstetricians and Gynaecologists, Royal Society (*1983*)

The 1983 BMA and RCOG statements each supported the MRC guidelines but differed in their specification of how long embryos used for research might be allowed to develop. The BMA (justifying the use of 'spare' embryos in terms of maximising the effectiveness and minimising risks of *in vitro* fertilisation therapy) argued that 'observations' on the embryo should 'normally be completed within five to ten days and always within a maximum of fourteen days of fertilisation'.[56] The RCOG (mentioning also wider medical research and therapeutic ends) argued that the embryo 'should not be allowed to develop beyond the stage of early neural development' which it identified as 'Day 17 after conception'.[57] In contrast to the BMA and RCOG, however, the Royal Society's submission to the Warnock Committee was reluctant to specify a time limit. Some forms of research, it stated, might involve prolonged culture of an early embryo, without entailing 'formation of organised tissue of the type found in the definitive embryo' (i.e. the cells 'which will eventually become the fetus' as opposed to the 'extra-embryonic tissues that initiate and maintain interaction with the mother'). There were also other experiments in which study of viruses or drugs causing foetal malfunction might require 'the use of embryos in which organisation of the definitive embryo had begun'. In these cases, the Royal Society argued, 'the value of the information to be gained from particular experiments should be taken into account when their acceptability is being assessed and their end-point decided'.[58]

Council for Science and Society Working Party (*1984*)

An argument similar to that of the Royal Society was advanced by the CSS Working Party, which held that, 'each use' of embryos 'requires its own justification in the light of its potential benefits'. However, the Working Party believed that 'it would be unethical for fetuses to be used at, or beyond, the stage at which their developing nervous systems might be sufficient to provide them with some rudimentary sense of awareness'.[59] Its thinking on this, the Working Party stated, had 'been much influenced by the virtual certainty that there is no possibility of even the most rudimentary "awareness" in the embryo or fetus until its physiological system has become sufficiently developed and has given rise to an organised nervous system'. The Working Party concluded that 'the issues probably reduce to the rightness of experimentation on spare embryos up to about the second week'.[60]

Medical Research Council (*1985*)

The MRC's 1985 Response to the Warnock Report shared some of the Royal Society's doubts about a specified time limit. The fourteen-day limit proposed by Warnock, it believed, would be difficult for an inspectorate to monitor; and 'because of variations in the rate of development of the embryo', there were 'advantages in specifying the limit in terms of stages of development [as its own 1982 guidelines had done] rather than days after fertilisation'. The MRC, in common with the RCOG, the Royal Society and CSS Working Party, also differed from Warnock by arguing that such limitations should not be embodied in statute.[61] On the other hand, the RCOG[62] and the CSS Working Party[63] had proposed, and the MRC agreed, that a statutory licensing authority of the kind recommended by Warnock should be created. Under such a body (and pending legislation the MRC and the RCOG set up their own voluntary Licensing Authority) a relevant code of practice 'could be subject to periodic revision ... to take account both of the state of knowledge in the field and of public opinion'.[64]

Surrogacy

On most other matters discussed by the Warnock Committee there was broad agreement between Warnock's recommendations and those of the MRC, BMA, RCOG, and CSS Working Party. However, on the question of surrogate motherhood, while all the bodies which mentioned it wished to discourage it, the BMA[65] and RCOG[66] did not go so far as Warnock's recommendation that it be rendered criminal, and the CSS Working Party actively discouraged this: 'womb-leasing' contracts, it believed, were at present unenforceable, but so too, probably, would be any law to prohibit them. The Working Party (agreeing in advance with one of Warnock's dissenting minorities), also argued that 'the procedure *might* be justifiable in very exceptional circumstances'.[67]

Dissent: Royal College of General Practitioners (1983)

Within the general area of agreement between Warnock and the professional and scientific bodies, a dissenting note was struck by the RCGP. A submission to the Warnock Committee prepared by a RCGP Working Party stated that IVF, including the creation of spare embryos, was 'ethically acceptable'.[68] But it stated also that both the freezing of human embryos, and their experimental use were unethical. Such experiments, it argued, however potentially beneficial, were comparable to 'unethical experiments such as those performed on human subjects during the last World War'. From the moment of fertilisation, the RCGP Working Party argued, 'the embryo should be treated with respect and experimentation on human embryos should be subject to the same ethical considerations as on children and adults'.[69]

These conclusions were subsequently disputed by a minority of the members of the RCGP Council, who 'were worried that if all experimentation on human embryos were abolished, important advances in medical care might be delayed or not achieved at all'. This concern was noted in a covering letter from the RCGP Council, which confined its full endorsement to its Working Party's recommendations for a regulatory body. The letter also reaffirmed 'the College's view on abortion, which is that it should continue to be available'.[70]

Arguments on research: MRC, RCGP

The RCGP, MRC and BMA stated rather than argued their
ethical conclusions on embryo research. The MRC (admitting
that some members of its own Advisory Group on the subject
had 'hesitations' similar to those of Warnock's minority) concluded in its 1985 Response that 'the generation of embryos
for and during research was necessary, and acceptable in the
public interest': in defence of this conclusion it simply noted
the potential benefits of such research in the diagnosis and
treatment of infertility and in relation to congenital and
chromosomal abnormalities and to contraception.[71] The RCGP
Working Party, on the other hand, based its opposition to such
research, however potentially beneficial, on the statement that
'although there are conflicting views about the onset of human
life, the process can be considered to commence at fertilisation,
since this is the point at which a genetically complete embryo is
formed'.[72]

Argument: RCOG, CSS Working Party

The RCOG and the CSS Working Party examined arguments
for and against embryo research in greater detail. Both found
difficulties with the claim that the embryo should be given
'absolute protection' because a unique, individual, genetically
coded human life 'begins at conception'. This claim seemed at
odds with the Western moral tradition, in which, the RCOG
noted, 'human status was attributed and protection was accorded, as physical development warranted recognition; and the
protection became stronger as the fetus advanced stage by stage
towards maturity and birth'.[73] It was only in the nineteenth
century, the CSS Working Party observed, that absolute inviolability from conception began to be claimed, largely because the
Roman Catholic Church was alarmed by the consequences of
new medical techniques which made early abortion safer.[74] And
society today, 'by allowing abortion under certain circumstances', did not seem to accept the claim.[75]

Nature, as well as society, suggested reasons for doubting the
absolutist claim. 'Knowing as we do', the RCOG remarked,

'that in the natural process large numbers of fertilised ova are lost before implantation, it is morally unconvincing to claim inviolability for an organism with which nature itself is so prodigal'. The 'physical question' of life's beginning, moreover, was 'by no means simple'. Conception itself was 'a process with demarcation points at fertilisation and implantation': before fertilisation there was 'the independent life of sperm and ovum', after it the possibility, for example, of a hydatidiform mole.[76] There was, also, the CSS Working Party pointed out, the possibility of the embryo dividing to form twins or, more rarely, of the two parts reuniting. Such considerations made it implausible to claim that an individual human soul (in traditional terms the ground for claiming protection) was present from fertilisation.[77]

The 'status of the embryo in our scale of values', the RCOG commented, could not be determined by an over-simplified answer to the question 'When does life begin?' The 'proper moral question' rather was, 'At what point in the development of the embryo do we attribute to it the protection due to a human being?' This question could be answered only by 'human conscience or reason' taking account of the moral tradition and making a judgement related to the embryo's 'growth, especially its neural development'.[78] Such moral judgements 'in so rapidly developing a field', the CSS Working Party added, could only be 'at best interim judgements'.[79]

The Churches: artificial insemination

Modern church statements on AI began as early as 1897, when the Roman Holy Office, in reply to a query, stated that 'artificial insemination of a woman' was 'not lawful'.[80] In the present century, the subject was discussed in three addresses (1949, 1951, and 1956) by Pope Pius XII and in the Report of an Anglican Commission (1948). Committees of the Churches again issued statements on AI in connection with the deliberations of the Feversham and Warnock Committees, and prior to Warnock the subject was discussed in the Report of a Working Party on which the Churches of England and Scotland were each represented.

Pope Pius XII (*1949, 1951 and 1956*)

In an address to the Fourth International Congress of Catholic Doctors (1949), Pope Pius XII condemned AID 'unconditionally'. In the case of the unmarried, he stated, the reasons were obvious: marriage alone safeguarded the dignity and well-being of husband and wife, and the child would clearly be illegitimate. But AID within marriage was 'equally immoral', because the husband and wife's 'reciprocal right over each other's body' was 'exclusive and inalienable': it was, moreover, in the child's interest that his care and upbringing be the responsibility of those with whom he had 'a bond of descent' and who shared 'the moral and legal bonds' of marriage and parenthood.

In the case of AIH, the Pope stated, 'the principles of natural law applied': neither attaining a desired result, nor the goodness of the desire made AIH right – the end did not justify the means. The 'act of procreating' truly achieved its ends only when 'carried out according to the will and plan of the Creator'. Further, there was no question of AIH making 'valid a marriage between persons who are incapable of contracting marriage because of the impediment of impotence'. And following that, the Pope added (in a reference to the role of masturbation in AIH), 'it is never permissible to obtain semen by unnatural acts'.[81]

'Assisted insemination'.   In condemning AI, Pope Pius XII made clear that he was not saying that 'new methods must ... be excluded *a priori* because they are new'. He did not necessarily proscribe, for example, 'certain artificial means of facilitating the natural act or of helping its fulfilment when normally carried out'.[82] This was a reference, it was later explained, to 'what is termed "assisted insemination", whereby after the natural act of intercourse the husband's seed is projected from the vagina into the uterus'.[83] ('The semen should not be removed from the vagina, but a doctor may use a syringe to collect the semen and to deposit it at the entrance of the cervical canal.')[84] What made this acceptable was not only that masturbation (as in AIH) was absent, but also that natural intercourse took place. Moreover, the objection to masturbation was not to the sexual pleasure involved; no less unacceptable, Roman Catholic commentators

have added, would be 'the extraction of seed by needle, without any sexual pleasure involved, from the testicles of a husband for implantation in the cervical canal of his wife'.[85]

The procreative and the personal. The possibility of 'assisted insemination' apart, Pope Pius XII was anxious to make the point (as he put it in his 1951 Address to the Congress of the Italian Catholic Union of Midwives) that to 'reduce cohabitation and the conjugal act to a simple organic function for the transmission of seed would be converting the home, the sanctuary of the family, into a mere biological laboratory'.[86] This point was underlined (in his 1956 Address to the Second World Congress on Fertility and Sterility) when the Pope emphasised that the union from which a child is born 'in its fullest expression should consist of organic functions bound up with tender feelings and inspired by an unselfish spiritual love'. It was 'never right deliberately to separate the different aspects of marital union to the point of excluding positively either its procreative purpose or the personal relationship of husband and wife'.[87]

The Archbishop's Commission (1948)

In 1945, the Archbishop of Canterbury set up a Commission to study the 'theological, moral, social, psychological and legal implications' of AI. Reporting in 1948, the Commission approved the practice of AIH, but not AID, which it judged 'to be wrong in principle and contrary to Christian standards'. The 'evils necessarily involved' in AID, it believed, were 'so grave' that it should be made a criminal offence.[88]

Psychological and social aspects. In rejecting AID, the Commission doubted neither the integrity and motives of its medical practitioners, nor the emotional and social benefits to couples assisted by it. Moreover, AID was too new, and the secrecy surrounding it too great, for there to be any reliable evidence of its long-term consequences. But the Commission believed that the secrecy in particular was potentially harmful, both to children and to marital and social relationships. Reflecting current debate, it was also concerned about eugenic breeding schemes and the risks of and to donors who might 'sire excessive numbers of children'.[89]

The law. The legal advice accepted by the Commission was that 'where there is the giving and receiving of seed, there is the act of intercourse': AID was thus 'not only in the eyes of the law but for the common sense of mankind, an act of adultery'.[90] (One dissenting member of the Commission – W. R. Matthews, the Dean of St Paul's – criticised this as 'crassly materialistic', since AID lacked 'the spiritual elements which constituted the sin of adultery', especially the 'violation of a relation of trust between two persons'.)[91] The lawyers advising the Commission also viewed, 'as a matter of the utmost gravity', published information that some medical practitioners 'demanded' registration of AID children as those of the husband. This would be a criminal offence under the Perjury Act 1911;[92] and in the lawyers' view, because secrecy was 'of the essence of AID', any development of the law to accommodate legal registration would be 'impractical', contradicting the 'plain and overriding duty to avoid dishonesty and falsehood'.[93]

Theological arguments: 'Assisted Insemination' and AIH. Like Pope Pius XII, the Commission discussed theological arguments about the purposes of marriage and sexual intercourse, but unlike the Pope it was willing (with one member – R. C. Mortimer, the Bishop of Exeter – dissenting) to approve AIH as well as 'assisted insemination'. A natural-law argument based on 'the internal structure and inherent purpose'[94] of the sexual organs was considered but not deployed against AIH: in AIH, it was argued, masturbation, 'the act which produces the seminal fluid, being in this instance directed towards the completion (impossible without it) of the procreative end of marriage, loses its character of self-abuse'.[95]

AID: the personal and the procreative. The Commission's theological argument against AID was based on the purposes of marriage – procreation, union and 'society, help and comfort'. Since the Lambeth Conference of 1930 had decided that contraception might be justified by circumstances, the Commission could not argue, with the Pope, on the grounds that the unitive and procreative should never be separated. Indeed it argued that it was not wrong for 'a sexual act within marriage' on 'the great majority of occasions' to serve only one of the purposes, and that 'for the theologian, Catholic or Protestant, the unitive would seem to be paramount'.[96] But in the case of AID, the unitive, personal relationship was eliminated. AID extracted 'procreation entirely from the nexus of human relationships, in or outside of marriage'. It represented, in effect, 'the prostitution, not of a class of women, but of womanhood itself – which is thenceforth valued less for personal than for explicitly sexual qualities'.[97]

Inordinate desire. A further theological point made by the Commission was that if the desire for a child of her own was so great as to impel 'a wife to become the mother of a child who is not her husband's, this desire was 'in strict truth *inordinate*: one which exceeds the proper bounds of desire'. On 'what rational ground', the Commission asked, was 'it urged that while *sexual* desires might not be exercised at will, *parental* desires may be?' To accede to this desire was to 'reject in principle ... the very idea of limitation, acceptance, of a given natural order and social frame – in a word, of the creatureliness of man'.[98]

The Christian Ethic. In dissenting from the Commission's conclusions about AID, the Dean of St Paul's suggested that AID should be considered 'from the standpoint of the Christian ethic', which 'springs from the one central conviction that God is love' rather than from the 'stoic' one 'of a "law of nature", which, as Bishop Butler pointed out, may lend itself to many interpretations'. (The fertile wife of an infertile man, for example, might argue that since her reproductive system was 'for the end of bearing children', it was not only right but her duty 'to have children by another man, whether by natural intercourse or by AID'.) The 'static view' of the Commission's theological reasoning, assuming 'that the form of the family must remain pretty much as it is', ignored Jesus' own criticisms of the family. Christians, the Dean believed, 'ought not to identify their religion with things as they are, even in the case of the family. Like all human things, it will change'. What mattered was to judge by 'the Christian law of love' whether 'the

employment of any mechanical aids to procreation strikes a
blow at the integrity of the human personality and the intimate
union of body, mind and spirit'.[99]

Feversham submissions: Anglican (1959)

A decade later, when the Church of England came to submit
evidence to the Feversham Committee, the Committee appointed
by the Archbishop of Canterbury for this purpose adopted the
main finding of the 1948 Commission, holding 'AID to be
wrong on theological, moral and social grounds'.[100] (This Committee was chaired by the Bishop of Exeter, R. C. Mortimer,
who in the meantime had withdrawn his objection to AIH.
But it also had one dissenting member – Mr J. Wren-Lewis –
who maintained objections similar to those of the Dean of St
Paul's.) The Committee's conclusions were approved by the
Archbishop of Canterbury, albeit with the qualification that 'for
my own part ... I desire to see the practice [of AID] prohibited
by law'.[101]

Laws and liberties.   The Archbishop's Committee had not been
'in favour of increasing the number of criminal offences'. Such
legislation, it believed was 'not required, provided it is made
clear that in law the practice of AID is on the same footing as
adultery or fornication'. The law, the Committee explained,
recognised not only rights and prohibitions, but also 'mere
liberties'. An example of these was fornication,[102] which no one
had a right to indulge in, but which was not of itself prohibited
in law. Adultery, while 'unlawful without being a crime', was
nevertheless 'a civil wrong giving rise to remedies in the courts
for the benefit of the innocent spouse who has in no way
consented to the act'. This category, the Committee believed,
could be stated so as to include AID.[103]

Registration and regulation.   The Archbishop's Committee was
concerned also that the law on truthful registration of births
should be restated or strengthened to emphasise that it was
wrong to enter an AID child 'as the offspring of the woman's
husband'. It hoped strongly that its recommendations would be
accepted by the Feversham Committee. But if they were not and

AID was to be regarded as lawful, the Committee believed that it should be regulated by 'an appropriate medical authority' such as the RCOG, or in the last resort by law. Matters governed by such regulation should include the circumstances of both insemination and registration, the selection and limitation of donors, and the obtaining of written consent from the woman, the donor and their spouses.[104]

Feversham submissions: Roman Catholic (1960)

A submission to the Feversham Committee 'on behalf of the Catholic Body in England and Wales', made by a Committee appointed by the Cardinal Archbishop of Westminster, followed the teaching of Pope Pius XII in rejecting both AID and AIH (but not 'assisted insemination'). The theological principles on which this judgement were based were again those of natural law: first, that 'the manner in which human faculties work indicates the ends which they are meant to serve, and also the means by which these are to be attained': and second, that 'the end cannot justify the means'.[105]

A false analogy. Applying the first of these principles to AI, the Committee criticised a false analogy between 'the generative faculty' and 'other faculties such as sight and hearing'. 'Accidental deficiencies' in the working of the latter rightly might be made up artificially by, say, spectacles or hearing aids, because these faculties were 'means to the individual good of their possessor'. But the generative faculty was 'not designed primarily and directly for the good of its individual possessor'. Rather, 'the complementary nature of the generative organs, the mutual act in which they properly function, the procreative purpose they serve' all indicated that they were 'designed to be used not in solitary acts, but with another person and for the good of the human species'.[106]

Artificial and Assisted Insemination. Thus, the Committee stated, 'the design of the procreative function points to the moral obligation of achieving its purpose only by means of the conjugal act naturally performed'. This purpose was safeguarded by the terms of the matrimonial contract which gave 'not a right to children, but a permanent and exclusive right to perform together natural acts of sexual intercourse which are of themselves conducive to generation'. Couples thus had no 'right to achieve conception by artificial means', only 'to promote the efficiency of the natural means by facilitating the act of conjugal intercourse, or by helping it to achieve its effects'.[107]

Prudential and consequentialist arguments.   Against AID in particular, the Committee added some further arguments. In the absence of 'adequate follow-up studies', the statements of AID practitioners should 'be treated with considerable reserve'. The Committee itself believed that tolerance of AID would lead to tolerance of normal adultery; the 'policy of deceit' involved might 'not stop at AID'; doctors, despite their claims, were in no position to judge the 'character, morals and motives' of donors; secrecy was unlikely to be preserved and the truth could be injurious to the child and hurtful to deceived grandparents; the risk of consanguineous unions would be difficult to avoid. The Committee's strongest statements were reserved for donors and recipients. The former, 'prepared to function as human stallions ... connive with an unknown woman to violate her marriage vows, and if married they violate their own'. In the case of recipients, the alleged 'insatiable desire of a woman to bear a child of her own and the desire of a man to escape from a sense of inferiority' were motives indicating 'a lack of adaptive capacity' (on which AID itself would place 'further stress'), which in turn was 'the hall-mark of an inadequate personality'. Further, the Committee believed (in common with others at the time) that 'vaginismus and impotence, conditions for which AID may be sought as a remedy, are commonly neurotic manifestations, which would strengthen the suspicion that the recipients are not psychologically healthy'.[108]

Recommendations.   In view of the 'dangerous potentialities' of AID, the Committee recommended that it should 'be made an offence under the Offences against the Person Act of 1861'. Recognising that this might 'be judged to be impractical', it urged 'that the law should at least refrain from giving any positive support or favour to AID and those who practise it'. The Committee also recommended that the sale and banking of semen be made illegal, that successful AID or AIH should not alter 'recognition by law of antecedent and perpetual impotence as a cause of nullity of marriage' and that AID without the husband's consent might entitle the husband to claim costs and damages against the inseminator and donor.[109]

Warnock submissions: Roman Catholic (1983)

Two decades later, the subject of AI was included in submissions made to the Warnock Committee by a number of Roman Catholic bodies. These included: The National Board of Catholic Women;[110] the Joint Ethico-Medical Committee of the Catholic Union of Great Britain and the Guild of Catholic Doctors;[111] the Social Welfare Commission of the Catholic Bishops' Conference (England and Wales);[112] and the Joint Committee on Bio-Ethical Issues of the Catholic Bishops of Great Britain.[113] The last body also commented on AI in its *Response to the Warnock Report*.[114]

AIH. Unlike Pope Pius XII, the first three of these Catholic bodies were prepared, in general, to accept AIH. The Ethico-Medical Committee believed that AIH and '"supplementation" of normal intercourse' were to be welcomed in the light of the fundamental importance in society of marriage and the family'.[115] The Social Welfare Commission (unlike the earlier Catholic submission to Feversham) believed that AIH could 'be compared to assisting handicapped married partners to have intercourse with prosthetic devices'.[116] To the Board of Catholic Women, it seemed obvious that AIH did not have 'the same moral defects as AID'. Some members of the Board were concerned about 'the severing of procreation from sexual intercourse' in AIH, and about the depersonalising and ultimately trivialising effects of medical 'intrusion' into the marriage relationship: but others thought that this was 'outweighed in some circumstances by the joy given to married couples previously thought to be incapable of having children'.[117] On the question of obtaining sperm by masturbation, the Social Welfare Commission remarked first, that there were 'alternative methods' for those who objected to this, and secondly that it was 'wholly inappropriate' to apply 'the same term to obtaining semen for

the rectification of the marriage act, and to procuring solitary
and self-centred pleasure'[118] (an argument reminiscent of the
1948 Anglican Commission).

AID.   On AID, traditional Catholic principles were restated.
AID, the Committee on Bio-Ethical Issues noted, was 'a violation of proper marital and parental relationships even when
done "for the sake of the marriage" or "to give us a child"'.[119]
Prudential and consequential arguments again were added. The
Ethico-Medical Committee and the Board of Catholic Women
suggested that AID might have 'a destabilising effect on the
family'.[120] The Social Welfare Commission, realising that others
might not accept such statements in the absence of 'hard'
evidence about the consequences of AID, argued that social
policy had to be developed on the basis of 'estimates of
probability' worked out within an orderly framework. In cases
where 'the risks affect something as fundamental to human life
as the physical and social arrangements of fertility, and as
fundamental to the structure of society as the family', it
believed, 'the risk/benefit calculus must be particularly
cautious'.[121]

AID: unmarried and married.   Applying this calculus to AID,
the Social Welfare Commission argued that providing AID for
the unmarried would amount to supporting 'alternative families'
or 'institutions which rival the marriage form of the family'.
This, it believed, would both imprudently increase the strain on
society's caring resources and encourage 'a system where the
dice are loaded against the material conditions for children's
happiness'. By contrast, it was desirable that children's 'personal
relationships, sexual differentiation and social integration,
should be worked out in the actual setting (of the family) where
these are at their most intense, or are themselves the essence of
the setting'.[122] Even within marriage, however, AID might
intensify a husband's normally difficult problem of adjusting to
the arrival of a child: guilt and pain over his infertility might 'be
succeeded by an equally strong sense of exclusion, possibly even
jealousy'; and this indeed might be partly justified, if the wife
tended 'to identify with the child in a way which excludes the
non-parental husband'. Moreover, from the child's point of view

there was likely to be the problem of 'genealogical confusion', intensified by the fact that 'what should be a personal, social link ... is known to be a matter of wholesale provision (almost literally)'.[123]

AID and the law. Like earlier Church statements, the Catholic submissions to Warnock took account of the possibility of their recommendations not being acceptable in a pluralistic society. The Social Welfare Commission did so by discussing the alternatives to the legal prohibition of AID which it favoured. Strict legal rather than medical controls (as favoured, for example, by the Council of Europe) would be needed. But 'the relative ease of the procedures involved' made a '"do-it-yourself" facility a real possibility'; and 'the consequent requirements of supervision, inspection, regulation and protection would be either inadequate, or extremely burdensome, restrictive, complex and expensive'. The need for secrecy for example, would hinder monitoring of genetic information, while a legally approved system with a 'virtually unlimited supply' would make it difficult to resist pressure to provide AID for the unmarried or for eugenic selection on positive as well as negative grounds. Legal prohibition, the Commission admitted, was 'rarely successful': this was illustrated by 'the nearest equivalent of AID in the past, namely extra-marital intercourse'. ('Control or prohibition of AID', the Commission added, did 'not imply control or prohibition of extra-marital intercourse', which 'for obvious reasons' was 'likely to remain a minority situation'.) But the risk (by analogy with abortion) of legal prohibition leading to 'back-street AID' was not a compelling argument against prohibition, since the only way of totally excluding 'back-street AID' would be the presumably no less acceptable alternative of 'AID on demand and completely unregulated'.[124]

In apparent contrast to the Commission's arguments, the Ethico-Medical Committee noted simply that 'necessary safeguards consequent upon the permission in a pluralistic society of AID' included: that 'the parents have a right to official assurances regarding the donor's health, mental and physical and ethnic congruence, but not to knowledge of his ... identity'; and that 'the child must have the same right to knowledge of his genetic parents as is now the case with

D

adopted children'.[125] The second, if not the first, of these recommendations went somewhat further than the Warnock Committee itself was prepared to go. However, when the latter's proposals were published, the Committee on Bio-Ethical Issues expressed in its Response the least measure of its disagreement by stating that 'AID should not be available as a publicly approved and organised service'.[126]

Choices in childlessness (1982)

In their Responses to the Warnock Report, the Social Responsibility Boards of the Churches of England and Scotland each made approving reference to the 1982 Report of a Working Party on 'Choices in Childlessness', set up in 1979 under the auspices of the Free Church Federal Council and the British Council of Churches.[127] Like the earlier Anglican bodies, the Working Party had no objection to AIH, but unlike them it was 'not prepared to condemn AID outright': while some of its members wished 'to discourage, if not forbid' AID, the majority wished only to limit its growth pending more evidence of its longer-term consequences.[128]

Adultery: the donor's responsibility. The Working Party discussed various arguments for and against AID. Some members argued that AID, unlike adoption but like adultery, should be ruled out because marriage was 'a covenant-relationship between husband and wife, exclusive of all others, not only in sexual intercourse, but also in the procreation of children'. But others argued that AID could be 'incorporated within the covenant' and might 'in certain circumstances support or even strengthen it', because 'the full and informed consent to AID of both husband and wife materially altered the case'.[129] Some members raised objections to masturbation and others to the payment of donors. Against the latter it was argued that payment might 'prevent any problems of undesirable emotional involvement, such as inordinate pride in [the donor's] own genetic contribution to society'. On the other hand, the donor, while seeming to do 'a service for the needy', exercised 'no continuing responsibility for "the fruit of his loins"'. This 'deliberate separation of the responsibilities involved in sex, procreation and parenting' thus disrupted 'a set of relationships, physical, psychological and spiritual, which together provide a rich soil for human identity and fulfilment'.[130]

Secrecy and truthfulness. The Working Party's major reservation, however, concerned secrecy and truthfulness. While evidence of the consequences for AID children was still insufficient, the Working Party believed that it was potentially harmful as well as wrong to conceal from them the nature of their conception and also, perhaps, 'knowledge of their ancestry', which might 'not be altogether irrelevant to identity'.[131] It thus recommended that 'while the name of the donor should always be kept strictly confidential, AID children should, if they so request, be granted access to their records'. On the question of registration of births, the Working Party believed that the present wrong in illegal registration could be remedied by changing the law.[132]

Childlessness and vocation. The Working Party's remarks on AID were made in the context of its wider concern with childlessness. Here, unlike earlier church bodies, it was prepared to recognise the possibility that 'a Christian couple may have a special vocation to remain childless', even if they were fertile, 'so that the particular gifts and abilities they possess may be better used in the service of God and his Kingdom'. A similar vocation might be recognised by couples who wished, but were unable, to have children: in this way they might experience 'the transformation of apparent failure and frustration into new life and service'. Other childless couples, by contrast, might 'still believe they have a vocation to have children of their own': if this was so, they 'should feel free to seek medical advice and intervention to this end'.[133]

Responses to Warnock: Churches of Scotland and England (1985)

Among the Churches represented on the 'Choices in Childlessness' Working Party, the Churches of Scotland and England were to return to the question of AID when, in 1985, their representative Social Responsibility Boards responded to the

Warnock Report. While neither Board objected to AIH, they disagreed about AID. The Scottish Board (whose Response was approved by the 1985 General Assembly) believed that Warnock had not 'recognised sufficiently the real responsibility of the donor' nor fully resolved the 'serious legal anomalies' in AID. In any case, the Board was not prepared to support 'the unwarranted intrusion of a third party in the marriage relationship'.[134]

The Anglican Board, recalling use of this argument in its own Church's earlier statements, argued that there could be 'a proper development of Anglican thinking on matters concerning sex'. This might be seen in Anglican thinking on contraception, from which its acceptance of AIH seemed to follow, since like contraception AIH 'interferes artificially with the course of nature, and ... separates procreation from the act of intercourse'. A further proper development might be to view 'the exclusiveness of the marital relationship' in terms of 'physical congress rather than the giving and receiving of semen which is its natural accompaniment'. On this view, AID would 'import nothing alien into the marriage relationship', nor 'adulterate it as physical union would'. On these grounds, a majority of the Anglican Board agreed with Warnock that AID was 'an acceptable practice' which, for couples involved, represented 'a positive affirmation of the family'.[135]

AID for the unmarried

The question of providing AID to the unmarried (mentioned above in connection with Roman Catholic statements) was not ignored by the other Churches. The 1948 Anglican Archbishop's Commission, while not considering the subject within its terms of reference, noted that it had been shown to be 'not simply of academic interest' by 'the recent proposal to inaugurate in London a League of Bachelor Mothers, the avowed objects of which are to promote and encourage unmarried motherhood'.[136] The idea of AID for the unmarried was discussed also by the 1959 Anglican Archbishop's Committee, which believed that it should 'be treated as amounting to fornication'.[137]

The 1982 FCFC/BCC Working Party argued that to 'extend the practice of AID to single women or to homosexual couples

... would in principle be wrong'. It recognised that 'some one-parent families, resulting from death or divorce, in fact provide a more secure and loving environment for the children than some two-parent families'. But it did not believe that this justified 'a decision deliberately to create a one-parent family', since children were 'in general disadvantaged if they do not have both a father and a mother'.[138] The Warnock Report's acceptance of this general principle was not questioned, in its Response, by the Anglican Social Responsibility Board.

The Church of Scotland Board argued that infertility treatment should be offered 'only to married couples' and not, as Warnock suggested, also to other 'couples living together in a stable heterosexual relationship'.[139]

The Churches: *in vitro* fertilisation and embryo research

Warnock submissions: Roman Catholic (1983)

The Roman Catholic organisations mentioned above submitted evidence on IVF as well as AID to the Warnock Committee. In doing so they restated traditional principles about means and ends, about when life begins, and about the unitive and procreative purposes of marriage.

The significance of fertilisation. The Committee on Bio-Ethical Issues, for example, welcomed scientific advances in infertility treatment, but pointed out that not all ways of acquiring knowledge were unobjectionable. The basic principle here was that 'human beings are not to be used as mere means to the ends of other human beings ... even when those ends are as worthy and useful as the advance of biological and medical science'. In this context, fertilisation had 'fundamental significance' as the beginning of a new human life. Restating the Catholic Archbishops' position of 1980 (on Abortion), the Committee noted that the 'genetic code' came into existence at fertilisation and argued that each such new life was 'the life not of a potential human being but of a human being with potential'.[140]

Biological and theological objections. The Committee recognised that biological and theological objections might be made to this view. In terms of the former, it agreed that science did 'not yet speak with confidence' on, for example, whether monozygotic twinning was 'latently determined from the time of conception' or was 'a really original event both caused and occurring some time not long after conception'. But 'on either scientific hypothesis, one finds at every stage after conception a human life or lives to be respected'. The only exceptions to this were 'where grossly pathological conditions radically affect fertilisation (e.g. where the absence, inactivity or exclusion of the female pronucleus results in a hydatidiform mole)'.

Any theological objection that the embryo might not have a soul, the Committee argued, was beside the point, since the Catholic Church made no pronouncement about the timing of ensoulment. This, 'as the Holy See formally stated in November 1974, "is a philosophical problem from which our moral affirmation (about the right to life of the human being from conception) remains independent"'. As the Holy See had argued: first, 'even supposing a belated animation, there is still nothing less than a *human* life (as biological science makes evident), preparing for and calling for a soul for the completion of the nature received from the parents'; and second, 'it suffices that the presence of the soul be *probable* (and the contrary will never be established), in order that the taking of life involves accepting the risk of killing a human being who is not only waiting for but already in possession of his soul'.[141]

Humanity and characteristics.   While the other Catholic bodies assumed the same principles, the Social Welfare Commission offered an additional argument, specifically to counter a currently 'loosely agreed opinion that the development of the embryo's nervous system and the development of corresponding activity in the cortex, may constitute the basis of an entitlement to protection'. This view, the Commission argued, based entitlement on 'a set of characteristics acquired at a particular stage in the embryo's life, rather than on the embryo being described as individual and human as such'. But the dangers in this were that 'loss of these characteristics, if they are pitched at a high level, threatened to remove protection from human beings, for instance, in certain cases towards the end of their life'; and equally, if the characteristics were 'pitched at a lower level, they could be challenged, or claimed with equal or more validity, by non-human possessors of these characteristics, namely some higher animals – since, *ex hypothesi*, humanity is not the decisive factor'.[142]

Practices to be prohibited. Assuming its argument about the embryo, the Committee on Bio-Ethical issues believed that it was only consistent with the medical world's own Declaration of Helsinki (on research involving human subjects) that certain practices 'were fundamentally unacceptable' and 'should be prohibited by legislation'. These included 'any form of experimentation on' or 'observation of a human embryo' which might 'endanger it by delaying the time of its transfer and implantation' ('other than procedures intended to benefit that embryo itself'). They also included 'any form of freezing or other storage done without genuine and definite prospect of subsequent transfer, unimpaired to the mother', and 'any form of selection among living and developing human embryos with a view to transferring and implanting only the fittest or most desirable'. Such prohibitions would, for example, 'effectively rule out the maintenance of embryos in "banks" as resources for tissue- or organ-transplants or drug-testing'. Respect for humanity would also exclude 'fertilising human with non-human gametes or non-human with human' and 'all those procedures of sex-selection which involve the destruction of the embryo'. Similar considerations raised 'serious doubts about certain practices involving multiple fertilisation and multiple transfer of embryos'. There was 'urgent need' to determine how far these practices involved 'an unacceptable willingness to exploit embryonic human beings as instrumental to the survival of one (or perhaps two) in the set of embryos thus subjected to such practices'.[143]

A legislative proposal. Like the Committee on Bio-Ethical issues, the Social Welfare Commission wished to see such practices prohibited. But it recognised that the ideal of affirming 'the full status of person or human being which we ascribe to the human fetus' might not easily be enshrined in law, since society was 'at present incapable of agreeing when life begins'. In the hope, however, that it might be agreed that 'one should

err on the side of caution in the question of experimentation'
the Commission thought it 'desirable to establish a clear termi-
nology, a stable principle of protection which does not fluctuate
or become subject to pressure, and a legal/administrative formulation of a special status for the embryo at the early stages of
life'. Specifically, this 'status or right ... would exclude deliberate experimentation on fertilised embryos'. The Commission
believed that it 'would not seem to be administratively excessive
or impossible to require a form of special notification ... for
each "production" of fertilised embryos, with notification of the
outcome in each case'. A legislative advantage of this proposal,
the Commission believed, was that it would not entail repeal of
the 1967 Abortion Act.[144] (In the event, a proposal similar to
this was introduced to Parliament in December 1984 by Mr
Enoch Powell MP, in his *Unborn Children (Protection) Bill*, and
defeated in June 1985 by expedient manipulation of parliamentary procedure.)

Permissible IVF procedures. The Social Welfare Commission
believed that this proposal would not 'imply a total halt to the
IVF programme'.[145] The Committee on Bio-Ethical Issues also
argued that, after its proposed prohibitions, more acceptable
'experimental procedures to attain much the same scientific and
therapeutic goals' would be devised. Nor would these safeguards
'prohibit IVF procedures carried out with the settled intention
of transferring each embryo ... to the mother's womb, unimpaired, and at a time and in the manner most appropriate in the
interests of that embryo's future unimpaired development'; or
prohibit 'procedures in which sperm and ovum are introduced,
with or without prior mixing, into the womb'.[146] Such procedures also seemed acceptable to the Board of Catholic
Women[147] and to the Ethico-Medical Committee,[148] both of
which regarded IVF within marriage as broadly similar to AIH.

Procreation and production. The Committee on Bio-Ethical
issues did express some traditional reservations about IVF. Like
AI, IVF involved 'a severing of procreation from sexual intercourse'. In procreation by the latter, the Committee argued, *'one
and the same act of choice*, made by each spouse governs *both*
the experienced and expressive sexual union *and* the procreation

of the child'. In IVF, by contrast, there were 'irreducibly separate acts of choice, all indispensable, and all the independent acts of different people', none of which had 'the character of a person-to-person act of mutual involvement'. An implication of this was that 'the IVF child comes into existence ... rather in the manner of a product of a making (and indeed, typically, as the end-product of a process managed and carried out by persons other than his parents)'.[149] This 'relationship of product to maker' was one 'of radical inequality, of profound subordination' in which the child lacked 'fundamental *parity or equality with the parents*': 'products typically' were 'subject to quality control, utilisation and discard'.[150] Some of these arguments, however, the Committee admitted, were not agreed to by all of its members, and indeed went 'beyond definitive Catholic teaching'.[151]

Response to the Warnock Report: Roman Catholic

Criticism. In its Response to the Warnock Report, the Committee on Bio-Ethical issues complained that the Warnock Committee had worked with an 'unsound' idea of morality which focused on 'calculation of consequences', misrepresenting the claims of justice and human rights as 'strong sentiments'.[152] Moreover, Warnock had shifted the proper perspective of its inquiry from the interests of the embryo and child to those of the infertile, thereby making its 'primary concern' that of 'techniques for meeting an adult need'.[153] At the same time, it had apparently lacked the 'courage' to point out that IVF was 'largely designed to solve those problems of infertility' of which the 'commonest causes' were 'previous abortion, the use of the IUD as a contraceptive device, and sexually transmitted diseases'[154] (see chapter 6). On the question of embryonic development, Warnock's claim that 'the formation of the primitive streak "marks the beginning of the individual development of the embryo"' gave too much significance 'to what was only one stage' among others 'equally significant'. Much more significant, and unmentioned by Warnock, was the fact that the 'individual's genetic constitution, which will control all his or her development from conception to death, is established on day one'.[155]

Despite its objections, the Committee on Bio-Ethical issues agreed with the Warnock Committee that a new statutory licensing authority should be created to regulate IVF and related research. In a pluralistic society, the Catholic Church did not demand that its moral objections to IVF should 'be adopted as immediate determinants of law or public policy'. Nevertheless, legal sanctions should be 'focused most particularly on clear cases of *injustice*' ('destructive experimentation on embryos, or forms of observation and storage which are not in the best interests of the particular embryo'). Moreover, since public policy 'must not be regarded as amoral', even 'non-destructive' IVF was not necessarily 'deserving of support by public funds which would have to be diverted from other public health concerns and from other ways of alleviating infertility'. The Committee on Bio-Ethical issues itself did 'not think that IVF should be publicly supported'.[156]

Surrogacy.   One subject on which the Committee on Bio-Ethical issues did agree with Warnock was the latter's recommendation that surrogacy should be prohibited. The Catholic Committee had recommended not only that 'surrogate motherhood by ... "leasing" of womb (with or without payment) should be excluded' but that the prohibition should also extend to 'surrogate motherhood, by donation of ovum', 'surrogate fatherhood, by semen donation', and any 'parthenogenic or other uni-parental procreation by cloning'. The principle underlying these prohibitions, the Committee stated, was 'that children have a right to be born the true child of a married couple and thus have an unimpaired sense of identity'. More generally, it held, 'children have the right to be brought into the world in the context which tends best to promote their individuality and responsibility and their sense of identity and which characteristically affords them the most all-round and discriminating support in the crises of development and even of later life'.[157]

Choices in childlessness (1982)

Before the Warnock Committee was set up, ethical issues relating to IVF were discussed by the 'Choices in Childlessness' Working Party of the Free Church Federal Council and the

British Council of Churches. This Working Party, whose Report was commended by the Social Responsibility Boards of the Churches of England and Scotland, began its deliberations at a point when many of the ethical implications of IVF were only beginning to become apparent. It was clear however that a basic issue was the 'moral ambiguity' of scientific and technological means of dealing with the problem of infertility. While research and creativity offered 'possibilities for enlarging the boundaries of human life',[158] it was, equally, 'an illusion to think that we can engineer for ourselves a problem-free and pain-free utopia'. It thus was important to decide, positively and creatively, 'where to draw the line and how to achieve the right balance between a willingness and an unwillingness to accept what presents itself as a limitation'.[159]

Embryos and research. In this context, the Working Party agreed that '*in vitro* fertilisation of a woman's ovum by her husband's sperm, and implantation of the embryo at a suitable time in her womb' was 'an extension of AIH' which posed 'no moral problems'.[160] On the question of embryos which did not implant successfully, the Working Party realised that some people 'interpret this loss as the "death of a human being", and believe that the responsibility for this "death" is shared by those who participated in the experiment'. However, the Working Party itself believed 'such language to be descriptively and morally inappropriate': there was, it pointed out, 'a high incidence of loss even when ova have been fertilised in the womb, and we do not think of these losses as deaths'.[161] This did not mean that all forms of research on embryos were acceptable: 'experiments carried out to control the genetics of human breeding, as is already done with animals', the Working Party believed, raised 'far-reaching moral and human issues'; and while 'some experiments on "spare" embryos may be morally justifiable', others 'should clearly be banned'.[162] What was needed was 'an agreed code of practice, clearly establishing the principles and conditions under which this procedure may be developed and used'.[163]

Surrogate motherhood. The 'Choices in Childlessness' Working Party also believed that moral problems were raised by sur-

rogate motherhood and womb-leasing. In the former the carrying mother provided the ovum, in the latter she carried an
implanted embryo which was 'not hers at all'; in both the baby
was handed over to a commissioning couple at birth. These
practices, the Working Party argued, deliberately disrupted the
mother-child relationship, which was 'or should be, a con-
tinuously growing relationship, firmly rooted in the events and
experiences of the months before birth'.[164] Thus, 'whether for
monetary gain or not', they were 'demeaning to both mother
and child' and 'should be made illegal'.[165]

Response to Warnock: Church of England (1985)

Three years later, when the Church of England Board for Social
Responsibility responded to the Warnock Committee's majority
recommendation 'that the creation and operation of agencies for
recruiting surrogates should be criminal, and that all surrogate
agreements should be illegal contracts unenforceable at law', it
supported this, using arguments similar to those of *Choices in
Childlessness*.[166] (The Church of Scotland Board of Social
Responsibility agreed, quoting the *Choices in Childlessness* report, but adding 'that surrogacy differs only in detail, and not
at all in principle from other techniques involving a third party
in the marriage relationship of husband and wife').[167]

Theological division and inconsistencies. Other recommendations of the Warnock Committee received qualified support
from the Church of England Board for Social Responsibility.
The Board found itself theologically divided about 'the extent to
which nature is given by God with its ends determined, and the
extent to which we may regard it as "raw material" to fashion
for our own good ends'.[168] Each of its consequent recommendations was therefore that of a majority – accepting, for
example, the practice of egg donation in IVF, but not that of
embryo donation. As the Board's Response itself noted, it might
seem inconsistent to accept the principle of donation in IVF (as
an extension of accepting AID) and then 'to insist that at least
50 per cent of the embryo's genes should be those of one social
parent'.[169] But the separation of the unitive and procreative
functions of marriage, which IVF even without donation carried

further than AI, was already morally difficult for the Board to accept; and the practice of IVF for husband and wife was accepted by a majority, only because 'the number of couples who would deviate from the norm through the use of this technique' was 'too small a proportion of all couples with children to endanger the nature of marriage or respect for any embryo'.[170]

The status of the embryo. The Board's view of scientific research on human embryos was similarly that of a majority, and again the Board was not willing to go as far as the Warnock Report. Here too the implications of earlier choices were followed: as accepting AID implied accepting the principle of donation, so Anglican acceptance of contraception (including the IUD, which prevents implantation of the fertilised ovum) implied that 'while a fertilised ovum should be treated with respect, its life is not so sacrosanct that it should be accorded the same status as we afford to human beings'. This view, the majority concluded, accorded with the Western Church's tradi-tional attempt 'to grade the protection of the nascent human being according to the stages of its development'. While modern embryology no longer supported the traditional expression of this in terms of the 'distinction between an unformed and formed fetus', it nevertheless enabled the majority

> to make a judgement of value and believe that (on the view that the more probable view should prevail) until the embryo has reached the first 14 days of its existence, it is not yet entitled to the same respect and protection as an embryo implanted in the human womb or in which individuation has begun.[171]

Embryo research. On this basis, the Board argued, whether or not scientific research might be carried out on embryos up to fourteen days would depend on how 'worthy' were the aims of the research. It would also depend on the source from which the embryos came. 'To bring into being embryos purely for research and then to destroy them', the Board argued, 'would be to treat the origins of human life with scant respect.' On the other hand, to use 'spare' embryos was 'more acceptable' because research was 'only the secondary reason for their being brought into

being, the primary cause being treatment for infertility'. Even
then, the Board added, it was 'not clear that the use of human
embryos for research can be morally justified'; and a strong,
independent licensing authority would be needed to resist pressure to extend the boundaries of research unjustifiably. With
these provisions however, and by a majority, the Board was
prepared to allow research on 'spare' embryos up to fourteen
days.[172]

The General Synod. The Board for Social Responsibility's
Response referred to in the preceding paragraphs, and earlier
with reference to AID, was entitled *Human Fertilisation and
Embryology.* At the meeting of the Church of England General
Synod held in February 1985, a motion was proposed that

> This Synod approves that part of the Response of the Board
> of Social Responsibility to the Warnock Report which sup-
> ports its recommendation that research under licence, for such
> purposes as the detection and prevention of inherited dis-
> orders and the alleviation of infertility, be permitted on
> embryos up to 14-days-old, but it is opposed to the creation
> of embryos specifically for research purposes.

This motion was defeated by a small majority. Subsequently, the
Board for Social Responsibility published a further report,
entitled *Personal Origins.* This, while reaching similar conclusions to the earlier Response, discussed the relevant scientific,
theological and ethical questions in much greater detail, explain-
ing more fully the reasons for different opinions within the
Board's Working Party. *Personal Origins* was debated at the
General Synod meeting in July 1985 and a 'motion to send the
report to the dioceses for discussion, with the amendment that a
national licensing authority was essential, was carried'.[173]

Response to Warnock: Church of Scotland (*1985*)

The Church of Scotland Board of Social Responsibility was not
prepared to go as far as its Anglican equivalent. Its Response to
the Warnock Report stated that 'from the moment of fertilisation', the embryo had 'the right to be protected and treated as
a human being'.[174] Consequently, the Board believed that 'no

embryos should be brought into existence purely for research nor should research be carried out on embryos which happen to come into existence in the course of other experiments'. There should be 'an immediate moratorium on all experimental works which are not a part of treatment designed to improve the life prognosis of and benefit to each and every individual human embryo so exposed'. This did not mean, the Board stated, that it was opposed to IVF as such, which as 'a technique to relieve infertility within the husband/wife relationship' raised 'no moral questions'. Super-ovulation however did raise 'questions concerning the deliberate creation of new life without hope of its potential being realised', and the Board could not support the development of egg and embryo donation 'as valid techniques to aid infertility'. Moreover, the storage of embryos 'should be undertaken only to facilitate conception': embryos 'should be destroyed after couples indicate that they have no wish for additional children' or 'where the marriage relationship ends for any reason, or where there is no agreement between the couple over their use'.[175] A further, more general comment made by the Board in its Response to the Warnock Report was that that Committee had 'given no thought to the experience of infertility as at least partially a social phenomenon'.[176]

Earlier statements: contraception and foetal research. The Church of Scotland Board, unlike the Anglican, did not refer, in its Response to Warnock, to the implications of its earlier statements on contraception. In its Report to the 1984 General Assembly, however, the Board had sought to make a moral distinction between the IUD and 'the morning-after pill' by arguing that while both 'operate by the prevention of implantation of a fertilised egg', the IUD was a 'planned precaution', whereas 'the morning-after pill' was 'an emergency safeguard taken to ensure the destruction of any fertilised egg'.[177] The Church of Scotland's general position on contraception had been restated earlier, for example, in its Moral Welfare Committee's Report to the 1975 General Assembly: 'birth control within marriage is part of a Christian's response, both to the needs of his own home and family, and to the needs of a world where an ever-growing population puts an ever-increasing pressure on its limited resources'.[178]

On the question of research, an earlier statement had been made in the Report of the Committee on Church and Nation to the 1973 General Assembly. This considered the Code of Practice recommended by the Peel Committee (see above) and was 'in agreement with its terms'.[179] On the other hand, these earlier statements by the General Assembly were called in question by the 1985 Assembly's acceptance of its Social Responsibility Board's Report, not only on matters related to the Warnock Inquiry, but also on abortion. This stated that 'the "inviolability of the foetus" (1966 Report) can be threatened only in case of risk to maternal life and after the exhaustion of all alternatives'.[180] Almost immediately after the Assembly accepted this (by a narrow majority), however, the Church of Scotland's leading theologians in the field of Christian ethics publicly dissociated themselves from the decision.[181] A year later, after much debate in the Church of Scotland, the 1986 Assembly decided to 'reaffirm the position held since 1966, that the criteria for abortion should be that the continuance of the pregnancy would involve serious risk to the life or grave injury to the health, whether physical or mental, of the pregnant woman'.[182]

5 Discussion

Introduction

Turning again from public to less formal statements, this chapter records a further discussion by the group of professionals and laypeople already introduced. Their discussion of infertility was introduced by the gynaecologist, who had agreed to speak in particular about IVF.

The gynaecologist emphasised that her account was based on experience not in private medicine, from which the first reports of successful IVF had come, but in one of the limited number of centres which offered IVF therapy on the National Health Service. There had been as yet (February 1983) no births as a result of successful IVF at this particular centre. Because of this, and because the technique remained experimental, IVF was not undertaken without extensive prior discussion with the infertile couple, in the course of which it was made clear to the couple that the chances of being accepted for IVF therapy, and of its subsequent success, were slim. In this context, alternatives such as that of adoption were fully explored, even if it had to be admitted that the number of babies available for adoption was nowadays limited. Before being considered for IVF therapy, the causes of the couple's infertility were also thoroughly investigated. The investigation could include analysis of the man's semen, tests of the woman's ovulation, and laparoscopy (inspection, through a specially designed instrument, of the state of the woman's pelvic organs). These investigations might lead to the suggestion of alternative medical or surgical treatment. In the woman's case this could include surgical treatment of the Fallopian tubes, since blockage of these tubes prevents the eggs from getting from the ovaries to the uterus. In the centre with which the gynaecologist was familiar, selection for IVF therapy was restricted to women both of whose Fallopian tubes were irreversibly blocked.

If after discussion and investigation, the couples were still anxious to take part in this experimental procedure, the woman, if selected, would have to wait some time, the gynaecologist stated, before the therapy actually was undertaken. The procedure then was

> that she is treated with a form of fertility drug which stimulates the development of the ovarian follicles. She will have to attend the clinic each day for blood tests and for an ultrasound scan of the ovaries and, at the appropriate time, when follicular development has reached a crucial point, another drug is given to induce ovulation. In association with this she is admitted to hospital and the following day is given a general anaesthetic when she undergoes another laparoscopy in order to visualise the ovaries and to aspirate the ripened follicle to recover the egg.

The timing of recovery, 'before spontaneous ovulation occurs, when obviously the egg is lost in the pelvis', was crucial: there was in fact 'only a 70 per cent chance' of its being successful. If it was successful, the male partner then had to provide a sample of sperm, which was added and, if fertilisation occurred, the laboratory workers watched the fertilised ovum through a microscope for a sign of cell division. When this was seen, the fertilised egg was transferred back, through the cervix, into the woman's uterus.

Multiple ovulation

One particularly controversial aspect of IVF technique, the gynaecologist went on to say, was that, although she had described 'the way it is done in our centre, in some centres where the technique is actually being employed successfully – and that's something which we here can't claim at the present time – they're also achieving stimulation of multiple ovulations to be able to recover more than one egg at one time'. There were two reasons for doing this. One was that if two eggs were fertilised, there was a greater chance not so much of a twin pregnancy, but rather of achieving a single pregnancy. The other reason was that some of the embryos could be stored for future use, essentially to 'prevent the woman having to undergo a repeat laparoscopy, which is an expensive and potentially risky procedure, in order to give her a later chance of pregnancy should this one fail'.

Asked if these embryos were also being used for research, the gynaecologist stated that, locally, research was 'being done on volunteer patients: either infertile couples or people undergoing sterilisation who are quite happy to have the eggs recovered and sperm used for fertilisation, on the understanding that this wouldn't necessarily be of benefit to them personally'.

Infertility and venereal disease

The gynaecologist's comments on multiple ovulation and fertilisation were to provoke the second of two main lines of questioning and argument arising from studiedly naive questions by the GP; and both eventually converged in a discussion of the moral justification of technical advance. The first line of questioning was concerned with the causes of infertility in patients selected for IVF therapy. In her introduction, the gynaecologist had suggested that in the case of a not untypical patient, both Fallopian tubes might be blocked as the result of an earlier infection, or perhaps one might be blocked and the other have been surgically removed following an ectopic pregnancy (a pregnancy where the fertilised ovum is lying in the Fallopian tubes or the abdominal cavity rather than in the uterus; and where the risk of haemorrhage necessitates surgery).

Taking up the discussion with an allusion to this not untypical example, the GP asked the gynaecologist, 'Can I get you to spell this out? The main reason that the lady can't conceive is that her tubes are blocked; and the main reason that her tubes are blocked is that she has had in the past an infection of her tubes?'

When the gynaecologist agreed that this was usually the case, the GP asked further, 'And the reason she has had this infection is some form of venereal disease?' The 'most common reason', the gynaecologist agreed, was 'pelvic inflammatory disease, fairly often gonorrhoea. But other forms of infection too. It may be post-partum, it may be post-abortion, but it does imply usually that she's had some form of sexual activity that's led to this in the past.' 'And equally', continued the GP, 'although one might think that an ectopic pregnancy was an act of God, ectopic pregnancies are more common if you have blocked-up tubes, or if you have an intra-uterine (contraceptive) device?'

The gynaecologist accepted this point also, but when the GP went on to conclude, 'So, if you could prevent people from getting inflammation of their tubes, that would stop them getting blocked up and stop this expensive and complicated procedure?' the gynaecologist demurred. She agreed that 'the indications for this therapy are largely bilateral tubal obstruction due to infection' and that this was the problem with the majority of local referrals accepted for IVF. But she pointed out that 'there are moves afoot that other forms of infertility may be corrected by this therapy', and that infertility caused by tubal blockage occurred in only about 18 per cent of patients referred locally.

'The commonest causes' she observed, 'are disorders of the male. Female disorders are a third tubal, some of these, disorders of ovulation which we can very readily overcome, combined with quite a large proportion in which we can't find the immediate problem.' Only a minority of those with tubal problems, the gynaecologist thought, directly sought out help from specialists in infertility; and while among those who did there were 'a lot of demands' from patients who asked 'What about the test-tube baby?' the majority had to be told 'Well, that doesn't apply to you, that's not the problem'.

A final question on this subject was asked by a non-medical member of the group who wondered whether, in the case of tubal blockage, any consequent babies were likely to be infected by venereal disease. This question allowed the gynaecologist to add that while the infection 'results in very considerable scarring of the Fallopian tubes', it was 'a burnt-out infection, not an active infection'. It was, in other words, 'something over and done with'. Moreover, research in connection with IVF had

been very much to look and see if these are potentially normal, chromosomally normal embryos. By using this technique they have reduced the risk of abnormalities; and this research has all turned out to be very reassuring, in that children conceived in this way have a very good chance of being normal.

Suitability for parenthood

If what the gynaecologist had to say about the potential babies was reassuring, some members of the group found less reassurance in what she had implied about the prospective parents. The majority of IVF parents, the gynaecologist stated, had 'been married before – they've had previous pregnancies or abortions or unsuccessful pregnancies – on the whole they do have other problems'. This comment, which caused one doctor in the group to mutter 'Sociopathic', set the GP on a further train of questioning. Having secured the gynaecologist's agreement to his suggestion that 'by virtue of the lady's past life, previous marriage etc., she is going to be low on the adoption stakes?', the GP went on to ask: 'Would it be right to say that the girls who have got infections are likely to be in the lower socio-economic strata, that having babies is likely to be an important part of their life, so that they are more likely to be obsessed with being pregnant?'

The gynaecologist was reluctant to answer this question, but eventually conceded that it might be so. 'My feeling', she added a little later, 'is that so many people attach the ultimate importance to producing a child that, in every new relationship they have, at least in marriage, it's of ultimate importance'.

This impression of at least some candidates of IVF provoked the surgeon into commenting that such couples, who became 'obsessed with this idea as a sort of goal in life', were 'likely to mess up the bringing up of this child as well. Because of the nature of their previous history and social group, and a previous broken marriage, they will have a much higher incidence of having trouble bringing up that child even though it's a precious baby.' The gynaecologist was less sure of this however:

> I think that the couples who reach us requesting this sort of therapy have really been through the mill. They've been through the tubal surgery, they're still together as a couple, although one might doubt the stableness of the marriage. But they've certainly been through it, and it takes quite a bit to come along despite all that.

This defence of the couples was supported by the parish minister, who remarked that 'the people who shop at Habitat also have a craving for a child'; and when the surgeon replied to this by saying, 'Yes, but they'll get put on the adoption list', the Anglican chaplain began to express his anxiety about 'a group on "consensus in medical ethics" composed entirely of professional people making assumptions about working-class values and the value of those values. I think that's a thing that should not go unrecorded in our deliberations.'

Resource allocation

Although other members of the group shared the Anglican chaplain's reservations about some of the generalisations which were made in the wake of the GP's line of questioning, the considerations raised by his questions nevertheless provoked a number of them to ask whether the expenditure of time, effort and money on IVF was justified. The gynaecologist admitted to being 'worried a lot' about this. In discussing the importance of timing in the technique of IVF, the gynaecologist had already observed that, locally at least, the facilities were limited and the procedures involved had

> to fit into the nine to five working hours. There are few lab staff who are skilled in the necessary techniques. We are also dependent on nursing staff, theatre staff, anaesthetic staff. Now this may not be a problem in some centres that specialise in this, but if you're trying to run a service of this nature alongside the general services, there's obviously a lot of competition for facilities and resources.

Despite this however, the gynaecologist stated:

> I'm very much in favour of treating infertile couples. I spend a lot of my time speaking to infertile couples and realising the anguish that they're going through. But I realise too the disproportionate amount of time that this form of treatment is going to take up. It only takes five minutes to terminate a pregnancy – and the outpatient time. I'm not trying to make any judgements on that, but that can be done quickly. This requires an enormous amount of effort, time, resources – enormous resources that are really not available very much at all; and it's so remote for the majority of infertile couples, although they clutch at straws that it might be possible. Yet in the NHS, we're dealing with so many problems that we

really don't have the resources to cope with. I just don't know how you're going to allocate resources.

This *cri de coeur* from the gynaecologist evoked a variety of different initial responses from other members of the group about the justification of infertility therapy in the NHS. These initial responses focused mainly on how professionals and infertile couples themselves reacted to the availability or non-availability of such therapy. One aspect of medical attitudes to the subject, for example, was commented on by the Secretary who observed that medical students on gynaecological wards tended – when questioned about this – to justify the cost of expensive infertility therapy in terms of the needs of the particular infertile couples they had encountered, rather than by comparing the needs of these patients with those of others in different areas of the NHS. This tendency of doctors to think of fairness to patients in non-comparative rather than comparative terms, was also illustrated by the GP, when he stated that while he tried 'to conserve the resources of the NHS by not referring everybody to hospital', he did not see his job as being 'a filter for the individual patient'. In general, he tended to pass on decisions about resource priorities – mainly, he confessed

> because I take the line of least resistance. I don't want to have a lot of fighting with my patients: I'm going on looking after them. I may send them to the hospital, who will see them in out-patients and say 'Yes, we can certainly do this operation. But there is a waiting list of two years for it'. Which is what I knew before I sent them up. But one's constantly aware that there is misallocation, and not least that there's the hanging around waiting.

The GP qualified these comments by remarking that the part of the country in which he worked was 'exceptionally lucky' because 'we've got a lot of doctors to patients and so the stories one hears from elsewhere don't apply'. But in general, he agreed that if a service was available he would use it.

If the GP did not act as a very effective filter for the NHS, was it possible that demand for fertility treatment might be limited, further back in the process, by the kind of advice couples received from other professionals, in particular the clergy? Were clergymen likely to suggest to infertile couples, seeking advice, that infertility might be something which perhaps just had to be accepted? Or were they likely to encourage couples to seek treatment? The question was not one which the clergy in the group could answer. The Catholic chaplain confessed that the situation was not one he had met and, not having considered the problem before, he was not sure what he would say. Most infertile couples whom the parish minister met were older and, he said, 'You only notice it because they're often unrestrainedly fond of children, and you just think, "How sad!" But it's very rarely people actually ask about this.'

A filter of a different kind was suggested by the surgeon. Infertile couples living near a centre providing treatment, he suggested, would 'get drawn into the system and continue and continue', whereas 'if a patient in somewhere remote is told that they're infertile, then they'll presumably accept that'. This suggestion however was rejected by the nurse who, from her experience of rural Scotland, stated that infertile couples there could 'get very, very angry. They find it difficult that they are so remote' she said. In rural areas, the nurse suggested, the fact 'that, to a greater or lesser extent, we all find fecundity difficult to talk about' might be compounded if

> you have a GP who for his own private or religious beliefs is actually not fundamentally interested in sterilisation or contraception; and therefore you have a bunch of girls at one end of the scale who are desperately not wanting to be pregnant and at the same time, in the same community, you have girls who are desperately wanting to be pregnant. And how they together, in a small community, deal with that can be very, very difficult.

But it was even more difficult, the nurse said, if 'added is the realisation that somewhere it is all possible, and that one of the most important things is having enough money in your pocket to get yourself from where you live to where that facility – or even that source of information – is available'.

An additional difficulty encountered by infertile couples in remote places suggested a further reason for pressure to provide this therapy. It was 'impossible', the parish minister said, 'for anything in this line to happen confidentially in rural areas'. Agreeing with this, the nurse spoke of the distress which the woman of an infertile couple might feel when, having visited her GP about some unrelated complaint, 'she comes out and is stopped half a dozen times along the street and is asked, "Well, when is this great event going to happen?"' This talk of the 'great event', 'the emphasis laid down by society on childbirth and pregnancy', the gynaecologist thought, was a great obstacle to couples 'who might otherwise have come to terms with the problem'. Before IVF became a possibility, the gynaecologist said, 'we spent a lot of time trying to talk to couples and help them come to terms with the problem that really nothing can be done'. But now that the 'very remote possibility' of IVF had appeared, it was 'probably creating more heartache, because at the end of the day they may get nothing for it'.

A different reaction again to the question of what priority should be given to infertility therapy was suggested by the school teacher who argued that, in the light of Third World medical needs, 'many people would really laugh at a discussion like this'. This observation however was contradicted by the gynaecologist and other doctors in the group who pointed out that infertility and pelvic inflammatory disease were important problems in Third World medicine, particularly in Africa. Up to this point therefore, the discussion of resource allocation in relation to infertility had been largely inconclusive. More would be said on the subject later, but not before the group's perspective had been altered somewhat by further consideration of the technique of IVF.

Multiple ovulation and frozen embryos

The particular aspect of IVF technique which altered the group's perspective was that, already referred to, of multiple ovulation.

Returning to this subject, the GP said that, as he understood it, 'it was possible with drugs for the lady to produce quite a few eggs at one time, and to put these into a test tube and put in the man's sperm and then get quite a few fertilised ova'. If that was the case, the GP said, then 'obviously one lucky embryo is put into a uterus and lives happily ever afterwards'. But what happened to the other embryos? Were they aborted, or were they 'put into the receptive uterus of a lady whose ova they weren't and whose husband's sperm they weren't?' Replying to this, the gynaecologist stated that the idea was to reserve the other embryos for the particular couple involved, in case the first attempt was unsuccessful. 'But' said the GP,

> obviously it would be technically simpler if there were other ladies who had come to the right stage of their menstrual cycle, when their uterus would be receptive to an embryo; and this would be fairly easy to calculate without going through your laparoscopies and so forth. So if you had half a dozen embryos at the right stage you would pop them in?

Replying, the gynaecologist observed that things were not so simple. 'Potentially', the GP might be right: 'but', she said, 'nobody's tried it, because obviously there are immunological influences at stake, and nobody knows and nobody dares try it, I'm sure'.

This exchange between the GP and the gynaecologist obviously troubled the surgeon who, when the GP went on to ask how long the other embryos survived, interjected:

> I think this is what nobody knows. I think if one is to discuss an ethical problem here, it's not the ethics of tubal obstruction. It's the problem that there are maybe several hundred potential human lives lying in cold storage in Melbourne, which is probably the most advanced of the *in vitro* centres. I mean this really is Brave New World.

These embryos were not developing then? the GP asked. 'No' replied the surgeon, 'they're frozen at an eight-cell organism.' And so, said the GP, 'they can be warmed up, and then start dividing and ...' To which the surgeon replied:

> They don't know that. This chap in Melbourne has not succeeded in obtaining an *in vitro* pregnancy from a flash frozen embryo, but the potential remains. He's working on it. And he's been asked by investigative journalists what is the fate of these potential human lives – I mean very emotional potential human lives, because they're under nobody's direction; they're not like an abortion or a contraception where the doers of the deed decide the fate of the child.

So, said the GP, 'they don't belong to the father, they don't belong to the mother?' 'They potentially belong to the mother,' the surgeon replied. 'But they're lying in a nondescript fridge, in a nondescript container, with a label on it. It is a very frightening concept.'

This discussion, it should perhaps be remembered, antedated the Report, not only of the Warnock Committee but also of the Royal College of Obstetricians and Gynaecologists, on this subject. It also antedated reports of the successful implantation of formerly frozen embryos. On the question of the technical feasibility of using frozen embryos for IVF, the group had to rely, therefore, on reports of its success in veterinary science, which led the surgeon to remark that 'if it's done with the animals it's not very far away before it's feasible'.

The gynaecologist, too, thought that it was just a question of time. 'It's like going back to the old subject of AID. Sperm were being frozen for a while and it didn't work. But now frozen sperm is being inseminated all the time, being successful.' The gynaecologist's view then was that

> in time the possibility is that the couple will conceive several embryos *in vitro* and if the first one doesn't take, they'll come back for further treatment: the second one maybe not, but the third one may well have a baby out of it. And that's how I see it: that these embryos kept in cold storage are the property of this couple, although that's never been established.

This view troubled the Catholic chaplain, who observed that the third might not be the last of the frozen embryos; and when the gynaecologist remarked that it was 'something the couple decide', the Catholic chaplain replied that if the embryos could be kept alive long enough, the couple themselves would be dead. What would happen to the embryos then? It was, the surgeon added, 'a fearful ethical problem – the problem of murdering their own potential children'.

In the light of his earlier comments on abortion, the surgeon's view of this problem seemed exaggerated to at least one of his medical colleagues, who reported recently hearing a scientist involved in IVF state that

> some of his donors, parents, whatever, were quite happy that their four-cell, eight-cell, etc. offspring, if that's the word, be run through the machinery to see that the machinery's working, because obviously a technique like this requires

testing, and if this is going to be little Willie, there have to be similar organisms going through the culture medium or whatever to see that everything works; and certain of his donors have agreed to test the machinery, so to speak.

'Yes', commented the surgeon, 'I think this is the current let-out.'

Justifying biomedical advance

Discussion of the status, ownership and fate of the 'spare' embryos had revealed a series of moral questions. But the group was divided on just how serious those questions were. Some of the non-medical members were perhaps like the parish minister, who commented later in the discussion, 'It's part of the techno-logical society that us non-practitioners were just fascinated by the details of what you were telling us, all agog to know what you actually do.' Others, like the surgeon and the Catholic chaplain, were clearly concerned about whether medicine was 'justified in starting these experiments without having answered' questions such as those about the 'spare' embryos. The possi-bility of achieving consensus, particularly on questions about the status of embryos, was very difficult, as the discussion on abortion had showed; and on this occasion again the group pursued it no farther. Discussion moved instead to the broader question of justifying morally ambiguous biomedical advance. If what had been said about 'spare' embryos represented 'the thin end of the ethical wedge', the Catholic chaplain asked, 'are we allowed to start?'

The doctors hitherto most involved in the discussion re-sponded to this question with variations on a theme. 'The problem', said the surgeon, 'is it's now started and there's all these emotive people demanding the technique.' 'I think it's happening, I don't think there's any way of stopping it,' said the gynaecologist. The GP agreed, weaving the fantasy of how difficult it would be to stop such advances were they to be generously funded by 'a Gulf potentate, wishing his lady im-potentate to get pregnant'. But even as it was, he said, the gynaecologist's options were limited by her being 'a government employee, employed by the people to provide health to the whole body'.

To the Catholic chaplain, none of these responses provided an ethical justification. 'Because some people are doing something wrong', he said, 'doesn't mean that everyone should and can.' Nor, in his opinion, was 'the justification of the people the complete justification'. These remarks suggested to the Anglican chaplain that he and the Catholic chaplain were 'has-beens in the realm of morality'. The reason for this, he said, was because

> we've got to a point where ethical and moral thinking is actually retrospective, so we're not thinking about what will happen in the future. Things are happenings because rationality and technology dictate that to happen and we then invent a morality which is largely teleological and utilitarian to follow that up and justify it.

The Catholic chaplain however could not agree 'that technology can dictate morality any more than superior orders can dictate morality'. This, he thought, was 'a very serious question, comparable to the Nuremberg question'; and when the Anglican chaplain suggested that his idea of retrospective moral justification was 'not entirely unrealistic', the Catholic chaplain responded, 'Realistic in the sense of *realpolitik*, yes. But then you avoid morality altogether. If morality is what happens, then there is no morality left, is there? Right is might; and then there's no point in sitting here, is there?'

Motives and moral individualism

Not all members of the group, as has been noted, were as apprehensive as the Catholic chaplain was of these aspects of biomedical advance. Returning to the particular question of IVF, the gynaecologist thought that the ethical issues should be considered primarily in terms of the original motives involved. The motives, she suggested, probably 'were (a) genuinely to further science and the potential of science in relation to medicine; and (b) the demands of the population at large for this form of treatment'.

The Catholic chaplain agreed that this might be correct, but wondered in relation to (a) whether 'doing research for the sake of science' was not 'comparable to the problem that the atomic scientists faced, again perhaps a bit retrospectively. Because something is technically feasible doesn't mean it is socially, philosophically, ethically legitimate.' When another member of the group responded to this by saying, 'You can't undo knowledge. You can't actually put it away', the Catholic chaplain replied that he was not so sure. 'What', he asked, 'is the whole point of the anti-nuclear movement if not in a sense to cancel knowledge?' But some in the group doubted this. When one member suggested that moratoria on certain forms of chemical warfare, for example, had held, others agreed with the surgeon that 'the potential probably remains: it's just that it's locked away, like the eight-cell organelle'.

Accepting that this last point, about the 'spare' embryos, had to stand as an 'overhanging' ethical issue, the gynaecologist brought the discussion back to the second motive she had suggested. In the end, she argued.

> you can't get away from the central issue that for those individuals involved in this form of treatment, it is offering them something that they've always wanted, something that is terribly basic to human existence; and that is to reproduce themselves. Whatever happens to the embryos in cold storage, I don't think that you can deny that they belong to the individuals responsible for them.

The Catholic chaplain was not sure that the gynaecologist's point here could not be qualified. In her argument, as he saw it, she was 'working, as most of us have to in fact, from individual to individual'. But it was not just 'a question of a series of discrete decisions': the question also had to be seen in 'another ethical perspective, in terms of a social philosophy'. This view received some support from the Secretary, who compared it with 'the abortion issue, where a doctor may feel very sympathetic with each of the abortions he has to do. But in fact he knows that in making abortion more readily available, he is making it closer to contraception.'

The Anglican chaplain agreed, complaining that 'morality expresses itself in our society collectively as an extreme form of individualism'. In his opinion, this made the group's own concern with consensus in medical ethics highly problematic, because in contemporary society 'we're actually talking about individuals asking themselves what's best for them, and then saying, "What's best for me is right".' The Catholic chaplain concurred: moral individualism and 'the fact that we live basically in a utilitarian society' was precisely what he was criticising. However, when the Secretary suggested that the Catholic chaplain's criticism raised, in turn, 'the whole question of authority. Because is consensus in our society anything other than the aggregate of individuals?' the Catholic chaplain argued that the real problem for the group was still to get its discussion beyond moral individualism to a point where it was possible to ask such questions.

Society and 'shroud-waving'

One reason why some medical members of the group may have been reluctant to discuss matters other than primarily in terms of individuals, was suggested at the end of our section on abortion, in one of the doctors' implied fear of the loss of medical autonomy. Similar considerations lay behind the question about authority asked by the Secretary. A fear of a different kind was suggested by the surgeon when he argued that if society, as the Catholic chaplain wanted, decided 'what are the social and moral values', the 'society will bend to what are known as the "shroud-waving" disciplines'. 'Shroud-waving', the surgeon explained, 'is a cynical term used to describe the people who are able to get money with the spectre of death'. Advocates of renal dialysis often illustrated this, the surgeon said.

> Take the example of a miner who has worked down the pit heaving coal for maybe thirty, forty years. If he gets an arthritic hip, in Edinburgh he will have to wait three years to have a hip put in: anywhere else in the country it may be five years, unless he's got the resource for private medicine. He has given society a lot by bringing his coal out and he can't enjoy his retirement because he can't walk down to the pub; and he is not a shroud-waver; he is just part of something that society leaves behind and says, 'Isn't it terrible!' But if you get a renal failure wreck of nineteen, you will get the whole populace of the College of Physical Education to walk from John O'Groats to Land's End to raise half a million pounds to put that person on a kidney machine, for a life that

is of dubious quality for about ten years. And yet you will not give a valuable servant of society ten years happy retirement for the cost of a low-friction arthroplasty, which is about ninety quid.

In giving this example, the surgeon explained, he was not necessarily unsympathetic to many of the causes in support of which 'shroud-waving' was employed. Research into cot-death babies, for example, might attract money in this way and 'I can quite understand it. I've been to a cot-death funeral and it's the most tragic event I've ever witnessed; and people will rush forward.'

Nevertheless, the fact that what the Catholic chaplain was advocating – that society should decide 'on where we're going in moral and resource questions' – was 'already happening' made the surgeon question the Catholic chaplain's approach. Society's decisions might well be 'going the wrong way' because of the subject's 'emotive nature'.

The surgeon's fears about 'shroud-waving' were echoed by other members of the group. The Anglican chaplain, for example, had recently worked in a 'psychiatric hospital which was grossly under-funded' where 'everyone was contributing like mad, like the patients and everybody' to a fund for a regional CAT scanner, when 'any of that money on any of our wards would have been bloody useful'. Yes, agreed the surgeon, 'I mean a CAT scanner is a million pounds and the actual value of a CAT scanner is remarkably limited'.

But then, it was asked by several members, was shroud-waving of a sort not responsible for the irony that the gynae-cologist spent 50 per cent of her out-patient time on 95 per cent of her patients who did not want babies and 50 per cent on 5 per cent who did? Who was responsible for this? Was it the media? Or was it the gynaecologist's colleagues, waving shawls if not shrouds, who were feeding information to the media? In part, the gynaecologist thought, it was the media, but also 'I think it's coming from everybody. I mean this thing about having a family – the cot death thing is all part of it, isn't it? It's just so emotive. It's something that's so strong in everybody.' In particular, the gynaecologist said, the strongest pressures came from 'the most vocal in society', who 'would be the first to say "we don't want a child now, we're going to have it in five years,

even if it has to be a test-tube baby"'. Because of this, she
thought, 'the doctors are totally vulnerable. The patient says, "It
is not your place to say what we should do: it is our decision;
you do what we want."' The surgeon agreed with this. 'There is
no doubt', he remarked, 'that people do insist.'

Medical responsibility

The gynaecologist's apparent resignation to 'obeying the demands of society' provoked some other members of the group
to ask if it really was all so inevitable. The parish minister, for
example, asked, 'Is not being able to have a baby an illness
under the terms of the Health Act? What is this idea of health
that every British citizen is entitled to? Endless children and
unlimited success?'

These questions however simply resulted in the gynaecologist's
agreement: 'This is the tragedy isn't it? It's beginning to be that
people in the population are beginning to demand a perfect
baby whenever they want it. And it's just not possible. We're in
this unenviable position of having to supply it, which we can't.'

But was 'this unenviable position' not partly of the doctors'
own making? Was not the gynaecologists' problem, the Secretary asked, that they themselves had first said, 'We can do it'?
When the gynaecologist had agreed to this also, saying 'Yes,
we're trapped by having said we can do it, but we can't actually
do it very well', at least one of her medical colleagues, the GP,
was provoked to offer a reason different simply from emotion
and shroud-waving. It was, he suggested, 'wrong for the doctors
to blame the media or the people'. In the United States and
Canada, it was possible

> to arrange a hierarchy of doctors by earnings. Orthopaedic
> specialists and heart surgeons are at the top, paediatricians
> and general physicians are lower down, GPs are lower still
> and, not surprisingly, work with mental deficiency is at the
> bottom. Although we pretend in Britain that it's not so, I
> think it follows a similar pattern: the more prestigious the
> speciality, the better the payment, or at least the resources
> allocated. I think that often the prestigiousness is a medical
> decision, or if not a medical decision a medical consensus,
> evolution: more aggressive people go into the more prestigious

specialities. And this may change, in that orthopaedics may have been prestigious when there was a lot of technology in orthopaedics – gynaecology may become more prestigious in a few years' time. But I think it's not correct for the doctors to say that they're pushed into this by the public. I think doctors chase after their prestige, and the doctors set their prestige.

The GP's argument received some support from the surgeon, who agreed 'that driving ambitious people will go into prestigious things'; but at the same time the surgeon was puzzled about what in the first place had made these specialities prestigious. The Secretary thought that this could be attributed, at least in part, to the fact that the more 'scientific' specialities appeared to combine scientific and humane, effective and caring values in a way unique within the professions. He also thought, however, that growing public fears about the less admirable consequences of science had perhaps created a climate of opinion in which shroud-waving was less effective than, say, ten years earlier. Evidence for this he suggested, might be found in government attempts to reallocate health service funds to such specialities as geriatrics and mental subnormality, as well as to formerly less-favoured geographical regions.

At the end of this discussion of shroud-waving and medical responsibility, the Catholic chaplain remained convinced that he had been right to emphasise the importance of a social as well as an individual focus. Admitting that 'shroud-waving' was not a term he had previously come across, he said that after hearing it discussed, he thought he began to understand the nature of the 'emotive passions' which they were talking about. But precisely because such emotive issues were involved, it was important 'not to foreclose or foreshorten our view' simply to individual cases, but rather to tackle 'questions of basic values and social philosophy'. By bringing such 'emotive passion out into the open', he said, 'you make it possible to discuss it and modify it'. The Secretary agreed with this, but suggested a caveat. The fundamental ethical issues in resource allocation, as he saw them, were concerned with values in conflict. The fact that important values were reflected in passionate advocacy of the needs of, say, the elderly and mentally subnormal, did not mean that important values were not also involved in shroud-waving for a CAT scanner, or IVF research funds. Much of the problem, in his opinion, was that so often there existed a conflict of 'the good against the good'.

Lesbian couples and AID

The question of medical responsibility for the direction of biomedical advance was raised again in a later discussion which was primarily concerned with professional attitudes to homosexuality. In this context, the surgeon remarked that 'a minor ethical problem' might arise from 'the request of some lesbian women living together that they should have the right to accept either an AID donor or a surrogate husband for the purpose of bringing up a child between them, which is something which will obviously be denied to a male couple'. Such a request, the surgeon thought, raised both 'ethical and resource problems'. The gynaecologist agreed that this subject was important and should be discussed, although she was reluctant to do so at this point because she thought it complicated the group's discussion of homosexuality, by introducing questions about 'a third party and the normal standards of society'. Her own 'stand' however – or rather that of her colleagues and herself – was that they were not prepared to accept a lesbian couple for AID.

The gynaecologist's contradiction

The gynaecologist's position on this issue was immediately challenged by other members of the group. Were there not, the nurse asked, 'lots of children who had been brought up by two women?' There were, she added, 'many separated women who are doing fairly well and who actually produce a much more rounded human being'. The gynaecologist accepted this, but said that these women did so 'without any actual form of medical intervention. If they want to produce a child and go off and do it, then obviously society's not going to stand in their way in the slightest. But when it actually comes to medical intervention, it raises other issues.'

'In effect', the nurse suggested, 'you don't want to be men?' The gynaecologist was not sure if this was how she would put it, but conceded that it was 'something in which the medical profession are being directly challenged'. They were being asked 'Why treat us separately?' by two people in

a stable relationship, not really interfering in any way with other people – it's fine, they're very happy. Yet they feel that their lives are not fulfilled because one or the other of them can't fulfil her female biological role; and yet the clinic is imposing its own feelings and saying, 'You're not biologically behaving as we would expect.'

So, said the GP, 'Your advice to these ladies is "Although this act may be repugnant to you because of your sexual inclinations, go and get pregnant in the time-honoured way".'

The gynaecologist agreed that it sounded very much like this and also that she was involved in a contradiction, which she found confusing. 'I practise a philosophy', she said, 'where one tries to do very much what the patient wants you to do; and yet in this situation I'm not prepared to do what the patient wants.' In effect then, the Anglican priest asked, 'What you're really saying is that if one of your lesbian patients had got tipsy and gone to a party and got herself pregnant, you would terminate that pregnancy.' 'Only if she wanted me to,' the gynaecologist qualified. 'Yes,' the Anglican priest resumed, 'if she wanted you to. But you wouldn't have helped inseminate her.' 'I think I am saying that,' the gynaecologist replied.

Parenthood and upbringing

In defending refusal of AID to lesbian couples, the gynaecologist suggested that the problem arose 'when it comes to involving a third party'. Her mention of a 'third party' was taken up by other members of the group with reference both to the potential child involved and to the doctor of whom the request for AID was made. On the question of the child and its interests, the group was divided. The Secretary, for example, accepting the nurse's original objection and agreeing 'that many single women and grandmothers can bring up children perfectly successfully', nevertheless thought that 'it would seem more likely for the child to have a better upbringing if he or she had two social parents of different sexes'. Against this, the nurse argued that two women living together were not necessarily

isolated and might well have 'extended families of their own'.
The fact of having two parents of different sexes, moreover, was
no guarantee of a good upbringing: the children of busy
professional parents were often a salutary example of this. As
the single child of a manse, married to a minister and having
produced a single child, she thought she knew enough about
this. Later, when the GP had raised the question of educating
children about homosexuality, the nurse commented on the
general difficulty of 'handing on sexuality to one's children'; and
when the school teacher suggested that the way to deal with this
was 'by being as natural and warm and affectionate a father or
mother to that child ... I think it comes back to human
contacts. Affection, I think, is the balance to any deviance,' the
nurse replied that she did not think the problem was any
different for a lesbian couple. When the surgeon then remarked
that 'if you follow your conclusion logically then a stable
homosexual male couple should be allowed to adopt a child',
the nurse replied, 'Yes. I wouldn't argue against that at all'.

The nurse's argument then was that lesbian parenthood was
not necessarily against the interests of the child and that parents
of different sexes did not necessarily provide a better upbringing: 'the nuclear family', she said, 'can be the most hellish
thing'. This general view was supported by other members of
the group. While not necessarily speaking about homosexuals,
the Anglican priest remarked that 'quite a lot of bachelors have
adopted children' – or at least had in the past – apparently quite
successfully. Later, the Anglican priest said that he had

> been thinking for some time of a family in which a woman
> was widowed before her child was born; and she proceeded to
> bring up this child; and, galling as it must have been, he
> would describe other men as 'the daddy', particularly the
> nearest one. The solution in their particular instance was that
> she and her sister-in-law, who was also widowed, set up house
> together, these two widows, with two children. They made, in
> my view, a most remarkable job of bringing up a boy and a
> girl in a household of ladies; and the only relatives of these
> two ladies were all maiden aunts as well. So they were
> brought up in a totally, totally female society, a totally
> unbalanced society by any statistics. They both married early,
> married well and were prolific; and remained married.

Principles and probabilities

The Anglican priest's last comments were directed at earlier remarks by the gynaecologist and by the Secretary, each of whom had suggested a different argument for accepting much of what the nurse and others had said, but only as the exception rather than the rule. The Secretary agreed that all the stated alternatives to the nuclear family, including lesbian parenthood, could provide a good upbringing for children. Nor did he wish to contest various historical examples which other members of the group gave about the acceptability, to many people, of children being brought up by nannies or in single-sex schools. However, he thought that these examples confused 'the retrospective and the prospective arguments'.

> Retrospectively [the Secretary said] you can produce a lot of evidence that all sorts of unlikely things work very well. Retrospectively, when a handicapped person has been born and lived and does not want to end his life, you can say 'It was a good thing that that person, although gravely handicapped, developed into that wonderful person'. But it is still a difficult decision if you are faced, as a doctor, with someone who wants an abortion because the child is likely to have that sort of handicap. You've no guarantee that he is likely to develop into a wonderful character. I don't think that you can use the argument that because it has worked in that case, it is going to work in others. The doctor is making a conscious decision.

In considering AID for a lesbian couple, as in the case of abortion, the doctor's 'conscious decision' had to take into account probabilities and what seemed likely in principle. In principle, the Secretary said, 'I think I would prefer children to be brought up in a broader, extended family than in a nuclear family, because it seems to me that there's a greater possibility of variety and the extending of sympathies.' Because of this, the Secretary thought, it was unwise, again in principle, to narrow this possibility if it could be avoided. Thus when the other 'third party' involved – the doctor – was presented with a situation in which a couple wished to bring up a child in a context which seemed narrower even than the standard nuclear family, such questions of what seemed probable in principle must weigh heavily with the doctor.

Complications and uncomfortableness

These remarks, the GP suggested, seemed to contradict what the Secretary had said in an earlier part of the discussion, about homosexuality in general. In that context, the Secretary had argued that, in Christian teaching about sexuality, an important criterion was not simply whether acts were heterosexual or homosexual, but also whether or not they were 'personal' and 'loving'. Thus, although homosexual acts had often been condemned by the Church, the Secretary had argued, 'The real challenge to the Christian tradition is the possibility of homosexual behaviour that has the characteristics of a loving relationship.' Was the Secretary now denying this, the GP asked?

The Secretary argued that the criterion of loving relationships, and by extension a loving home, was relevant to the question of AID for a lesbian couple. Nevertheless, he still felt that 'the probabilities' had to be 'balanced against' this by the doctor. In principle, he felt, the question of AID for lesbian couples should be kept separate from that of the ethics of homosexuality because 'it was not the point on which the question of homosexual relationships turns'. But, intervened the Chairman,

> I think it is. Because I think that if we were comfortable with whatever the point is on which they turn, we wouldn't be worried about this question of AID or adoption. I think introducing the child into the situation focuses the fact that we are very uncomfortable with these relationships. We feel they are inappropriate for little humans to be brought up in; and that's focusing our uncomfortableness.

The Secretary responded to these remarks by saying that 'at an intuitive level' he was 'not totally convinced' by them. He found it, he said, 'increasingly difficult to see any fundamental objection' to the 'genuinely loving homosexual relationship'. If the Christian tradition did not reflect this view of homosexuality, the criterion of loving relationship was nevertheless also part of the tradition and could be used as a 'principle of interpretation' to justify a change in this particular case. He was, he thought, 'prepared to take this on board'. But he still found difficulty with the idea of offering AID to lesbian couples, and he believed his reason was the one he had stated, 'about narrowing the options'.

Society's view

In this, however, the gynaecologist proved to be making a different point to the Secretary. Although at an earlier stage in the discussion she had argued that because 'a child plays off the male-female role', then 'there should surely be a male input into the child's life', she later fully conceded that there was 'plenty of evidence that children brought up by single parents do very well, because of the concentration of care that they get'. Nevertheless, there was a problem about offering AID specifically to lesbian couples. At a stage of the discussion before the Chairman's intervention, she explained this by saying that because the couple were 'deviating from accepted family practices', then 'in general, society is going to be somewhat antagonistic; and this is going to reflect on the upbringing'. Later, after the Chairman's comments, she went further and said that the children

> were still being brought up in a society in which the norms of sexuality are very much towards the heterosexual relationship. People who are not heterosexual are still regarded as having a problem; and I believe most of them would still regard themselves as having a problem, although they can overcome it. And is it really the right of the medical profession to interfere in this process, where the natural process is for male and female to produce children?

The gynaecologist's question was clearly rhetorical. However, her use of the word 'natural' was not necessarily an indication that she herself thought that lesbian parenthood was unnatural in any metaphysical sense. In using the word she had been referring back to a remark by the medical student, that 'most of us probably feel that the natural thing and the only physiological way in which a child can be produced is by the union, in some way or another, between female and male'. The gynaecologist was taking this as probably the majority view of the society in which she worked, and her position on this was summed up by the Catholic chaplain in saying that 'an agency which has some sort of public authority shouldn't go too far away from the current public opinion'.

How much of public opinion this 'natural' view reflected was a point the group again was divided over. The medical student, for example, qualified what he had said by remarking that 'generalising from what seems to be the natural thing' raised real problems when individuals – transsexuals, for example, as well as lesbian couples – held sincere minority views about what was natural for them. The GP too wondered whether, in matters of sex and the family more generally, the majority view was as large as they sometimes supposed; at school, he said, 'my son is teased because he has two parents. In his class three people said to him that it wasn't fair he did so well in his maths test, because he had a daddy.' Against this, returning to the particular question in hand, the surgeon referred back to the Catholic chaplain's earlier distinction (see chapter 2) between explicit and implicit reason and claimed that

> there is an implicit reason in this room that a lesbian couple bringing up a child is wrong. There is a gut feeling that this isn't right: my interpretation of implicit reason is that it's a gut feeling. It's something inside; and we are foundering on our explicit reason, 'although all men cannot give a reason ...' I mean, we feel it's wrong for whatever reason there is.

Not surprisingly, the nurse disagreed with this; and when the surgeon said that 'the bulk of the group' had this 'gut feeling', the Anglican priest replied that the discussion, in his view, had suggested something other than this.

Reconciling contradictory opinions

A very broad range of opinion then was represented in the group, and in some cases even the opinions of individuals had seemed self-contradictory. Towards the end of the discussion both the Secretary and the gynaecologist attempted to reconcile their own contradictory opinions. The Secretary, for example, was again challenged with the discrepancy between his arguments on the one hand about statistical averages and on the other about the criterion of loving relationships. He dealt with this by saying, in effect, that a rule should admit exceptions: the decision 'in the case of a doctor being asked to give AID', he thought, was 'a question of policy; and a question of policy has to be decided by statistical averages and trying to work out what is likely in general terms'. Nevertheless, he said, the doctor could 'then be faced with a very caring lesbian couple, and say, "Well, in this case it's so obvious that it might be an exception"'. However, the possibility of such an exception did not mean that that the doctors should not 'be making presuppositions about what to do' in such a situation were it to arise in the future. They should try 'to work out their position on it, their general principles'. One reason for this, the Secretary suggested, was that the question involved resource allocation; and although, as the Anglican priest pointed out, AID was 'not the most expensive treatment', the question of selection for treatment, as the gynaecologist observed, was important because the waiting lists were 'phenomenally long'. A further reason was the doctors' political position: if public opinion really was prejudiced against lesbian parenthood, offering AID to lesbian couples might endanger the public funding of AID generally.

These prudential arguments, the Secretary emphasised, were secondary to his main point, which had been to suggest a general principle concerned with the child's interests on which policy might be based. Commenting on this, the Catholic chaplain agreed that some principle was needed here. The gynaecologist's position, that an agency with public authority should not diverge too much from public opinion, was, he thought, defensible. But public opinion changed and should not in any case be accepted without question. So principles were needed, although he did not think he agreed with the Secretary's, which seemed to involve 'a slippery slope'. ('Protestants', the nurse interjected here, 'are always on a slippery slope!') At the risk of being 'found very fundamentalist again', the Catholic chaplain wondered

> whether this extremely difficult case couldn't be regarded as the *reductio ad absurdum*: it's the logical extension once you allow certain things to go. I don't have to remind you, of course, that in the traditional Catholic position there has been this connection between sexual activity and procreation, how-

ever you interpret that. Now, could it not be said that once you sever that link, you will just make exception after exception after exception. And it's only when you get to the very end, when you get to these cells or whatever we were talking about that are on ice indefinitely, that you begin to see what was implicitly present at the beginning of the series?

Responding to this question, the gynaecologist tried to re-concile the conflicts in her own view. She saw the point the Catholic chaplain was making and accepted, she said, 'the connection between sexual activity and procreation'. But she also accepted that 'we've already taken on the role of interfering with this process to a large extent'. Was it not possible, however, to interpret this – in the case, for example, of agreeing to terminate a pregnancy – as 'interfering in a negative way', whereas the request for AID from lesbian couples could be construed as different because it was interfering 'in a much more active way'? She was not sure about this; the problem remained: 'I'm doing what the patient asks in one way, but not in the other way.'

6 Comment

'Moral judgements' and 'gut feelings'

As may be evident from the public statements noted in chapter 4, the discussion recorded in chapter 5 again touches on only some aspects of a few relevant ethical questions. Again, too, the discussion includes a number of questionable empirical generalisations.[1]

These demonstrate how what is believed (or predicted) to be the case may either contribute to the formation of moral judgements or be used in their defence. Neither the statements nor the discussion, however, suggest that the most fundamental moral disagreements evident in chapter 5 are likely to be resolved simply by disinterested scientific investigation. Indeed, when the discussion reaches the point of the surgeon invoking the 'gut feeling' that 'a lesbian couple bringing up a child is wrong ... for whatever reason there is', any hope of reasoned moral argument, let alone consensus, may seem to have disappeared.

Retrospective justification and Nuremberg

But is consensus on the ethics of AI, IVF and embryo research desirable? In view of the gynaecologist's opinion that there is 'no way of stopping' morally ambiguous biomedical advances (if these further science and meet 'the demands of the population') the Anglican chaplain may seem right to have argued that ethical thinking on these matters is now largely a retrospective 'teleological and utilitarian' justification of what technology has dictated. It may also seem right, therefore, for the Catholic chaplain to have warned that 'once you allow certain things to go ... you will just make exception after exception after exception'. After all, as he had reminded the group earlier, the question of whether 'technology can dictate morality', is comprable to 'the Nuremberg question' of whether 'superior orders can dictate morality'.

Consequences or principles

In the present century, clearly, no one should ignore the force of this comparison. Moreover, it might be argued, biomedical scientists have an interest in advancing their knowledge and in meeting the needs of their existing individual patients, and so may not be the best critics of potential abuses. The best safeguard against the Catholic chaplain's 'slippery slope' thus may be if bodies like his Church argue uncompromisingly for moral principles which are not 'teleological or utilitarian', but deontological – principles, that is, which state what is right and wrong in itself, whatever the consequences. Against this it might be pointed out that, since Nuremberg, it is the biomedical scientists themselves who have drawn up ethical codes and regulations to prevent abuses, and that the scientific pioneers of IVF and embryo research were calling for ethical guidance at least a decade before the Warnock Committee was established.[2] Nevertheless, even if this is admitted, the nature of this ethical guidance still has to be determined, and in this context the Catholic chaplain's argument merits examination.

An immediate problem about the Catholic chaplain's argument is that it too is 'teleological': it defends a moral principle in terms of the allegedly undesirable consequences of not taking a firm stand upon it. Considered simply as an argument about consequences, this is incomplete: it assumes rather than establishes that certain things are both consequences and undesirable, and it ignores other possible consequences, desirable or undesirable, of not taking or taking this stand on principle. However, these consequentialist considerations, while important, presumably are not crucial to the Catholic chaplain's main argument. In considering this aspect of the ethics of AI, IVF and embryo research, the most important question to ask would therefore seem to be whether the principles on which the Churches take their stand can be shown to be convincing in non-consequentialist terms.

Human faculties: ends and means

Two main principles seem to be involved in the Churches' statements. The first was expressed in its most general terms by the Catholic submission to the Feversham Committee: 'the manner in which human faculties work indicates the ends which they are meant to serve, and also the means by which those ends are to be attained'.[3] In this general form, the principle might seem a reasonable one to many people, provided that any generalisations drawn from it were made provisionally, and on the basis of scientific and historical investigation. On a common-sense view, it might seem the kind of principle a doctor might have in mind when advising his patient that the way his liver worked indicated that it was not 'meant' to deal with such large quantities of alcohol, and that the means to the end of his health or survival was greater temperance.

Natural law: two approaches

While this natural-law view may seem reasonably convincing in general terms, the problem (as the Dean of St Paul's reminded the 1948 Archbishop's Commission) is that 'a "law of nature" ... may lend itself to many interpretations'.[4] In the Church's tradition, there have been at least two divergent approaches to interpreting the laws of human nature. For some, like St Thomas Aquinas, human beings are sufficiently in touch with reality for their rational reflection on experience to bring them to some understanding, however imperfect and provisional, of these laws. For the Christian, that is, the idea of a 'law of human nature' implies a lawgiver – the Creator who implanted in mankind certain fundamentals which he expects to be discovered and respected, and which give rise to 'natural' duties on the individual's part and 'natural' rights or claims which he has on others. In addition to this more scientific and exploratory approach, others, emphasising the limitations of human understanding, have seen the laws of man's being as explicitly contained in the Bible and interpreted by Church teaching. This latter view is reflected in the Catholic submission to the Feversham Committee when, for example, it is argued that in such 'by-ways of morality' as AI, 'we would often fail to read the signposts of nature correctly and confidently were it not for the guidance of Sacred Scriptures and the teaching authority of the Church'.[5]

The procreative and the unitive

As interpreted by the Church's teaching authority, the general theory of natural law, when applied to sexuality, has taken a particular form in which the sexual faculty is identified as having two ends – the procreative and the unitive – of which the first has traditionally and until recently been assumed to be the more important. Contraceptive means which deliberately exclude the procreative end have thus been regarded as unnatural; and one shorthand way of stating this principle of natural law has been that which was employed by the Catholic chaplain, namely that 'the connection between sexual activity and procreation' should not be severed. Of course, this particular principle did not historically envisage the recent converse possibility of procreation without sexual intercourse. But when this possibility emerged, the tradition provided a way of understanding it. It was against the background of such ideas about what was 'natural', that the 1948 Anglican Commission was able to describe a woman's desire for a child by AID as exceeding 'the proper bounds of desire' and to equate this with rejecting 'the very idea of limitation, acceptance, of a given natural order and social frame – in a word, of the creatureliness of man'.[6]

Ecclesiastical retrospective justification?

To those who do not necessarily acknowledge the teaching authority of the Church, this particular interpretation may seem less reasonable than the general theory of natural law. The persuasiveness of this particular interpretation also may be diminished when the ways in which the Church has subsequently qualified it are noted. These may well be seen as the 'retrospective justification' of changing social attitudes and practices in relation to contraception, population pressures and new reproductive technologies. Moreover, retrospective justification may be seen in the theological reflection which has come to allow some emendations to the traditional interpretation – in particular the modern interpretation of Church teaching (albeit in a 'rediscovered' scriptural basis) – which gives the unitive end of marriage at least equal status to the procreative, and which emphasises the personal at least as much as the physical or procreative aspect of sexual union. This shift, it might be argued, reflects twentieth-century attitudes to marriage and the person rather more faithfully than it does those of traditional Church teaching.

The Roman Catholic Church's new emphasis on the unitive and personal has not led it very far down the Catholic chaplain's 'slippery slope' of 'exception after exception after exception'. It might be argued that Pope Pius XII's teaching on 'assisted insemination', which pre-dated this new emphasis, did not really alter the traditional interpretation by excluding either the procreative or the unitive ends of marriage. Nevertheless, the distinction between this and AIH (which in the Pope's view did offend against the traditional view) has proved difficult for Catholics to maintain, as some of the submissions to the Warnock Committee demonstrated. A further slide into acceptance of AID (for example by the kind of argument used by the Anglican Social Responsibility Board, about changing Anglican views on contraception as a model for 'a proper development of its teaching on sex' is excluded by the Catholic Church's rejection of 'artificial' means of contraception as unnatural. But the acceptance, also by Pope Pius XII, of the rhythm method as 'licit' again may be seen as paving the way for more serious emendations (such as the suggestion of some Catholic writers that use of the oral contraceptive to regularise infertile periods might provide the rhythm method with the secure and scientific basis for which Pope Pius XII hoped).

Authority and prudence

The particular interpretation traditionally given by Catholic teaching to the general theory of natural law, when applied to sexuality, would seem largely dependent for its plausibility on acceptance of the Roman Catholic Church's teaching authority. The only other relevant non-consequentialist argument which might have a wider appeal is that of the Catholic Social Welfare Commission (in its submission to the Warnock Committee). This suggests, as a principle for evaluating consequentialist claims, that when 'the risks affect something as fundamental to human life as the physical and social arrangements of fertility, and as fundamental to the structure of society as the family, the risk/benefit calculus must be particularly cautious'.[7] But against this prudential argument, even (or perhaps particularly) within the Church, it might also be argued (with the Dean of St Paul's in 1948) that Christians 'ought not to identify their religion with things as they are, even in the case of the family. Like all human things, it will change.'[8]

Killing the innocent

The second main principle involved in the Churches' statements, particularly about IVF and embryo research, is that it is wrong to kill innocent human beings. Stated in these very general terms, this is a principle which would seem highly reasonable to many people, not least on the grounds of self-interest, but also on those of justice and compassion. But here too difficulties have arisen, over the particular interpretation which the Churches give to this principle.

Fertilisation as crucial

One major difficulty is about whether the principle extends to according human embryos the full protection normally afforded to human beings. Public statements of the Roman Catholic Church, for example, have taken the view that it does, arguing that fertilisation has 'crucial significance', and supporting this with the argument that the presence, from fertilisation, of a unique genetic code indicates that there is a human life (or, if the embryo divides to form identical twins, human lives) to be protected. The crucial factors demanding protection thus are the humanity and the individuality of the embryo.

Embryological questions

This strong claim in defence of the embryo has been questioned on both scientific and philosophical grounds. Research in embryology indicates, for example, that not only is conception a process, including the stages of fertilisation and implantation, but that fertilisation itself also is a process, with several stages taking place over several hours. Moreover, from the stage of fertilisation to that of implantation, the fertilised egg, while in some cases having a potential for successful development (part developing into the foetus, most into the afterbirth), in other cases has no such potential – it will either be lost by natural wastage, in some cases at least because its chromosome complement is inconsistent with human development, or it may develop into potentially life-threatening abnormalities such as the hydatidiform mole. Since at least half of all fertilised eggs are lost by natural wastage, it seems scientifically inaccurate to describe many of these pre-implantation embryos as even potential human beings. If, then, potentiality is to be attributed to the pre-implantation embryo, it may appear at least as much akin to the potentiality of the sperm and unfertilised egg (for which protection is not claimed) as to that of the developing foetus.

Philosophical questions

Much of this embryological research is relatively recent, and its philosophical implications do not seem to have been fully assimilated in some of the Roman Catholic statements mentioned earlier in this chapter. Moreover, the traditional reason for according protection to the unborn is that they are human souls but the question of when they become human souls is one on which the Roman Catholic Church currently has no official position. The question (as the Vatican stated in 1974) is a philosophical one; and the historical evidence (as some Catholic and other moral theologians have pointed out[9]) is that the Church traditionally has made philosophical judgements about the timing of ensoulment in the light of current scientific knowledge. Scientific undermining of Aristotelean biology, for example, was among the reasons why the nineteenth-century Catholic Church abandoned the medieval idea of delayed animation or ensoulment. This particular historical justification of the traditional Western view that protection should become stronger with development, it was said, was no longer scientifically tenable; and the Church with its commitment both to rationality and to the protection of human life had little alternative but to drop it. A similar commitment to rationality today, some theologians argue, might lead from the findings of current embryology to a philosophical position, in its practical effects at least, not unlike that of delayed animation. This return to tradition might also serve the Church's commitment to protecting human life, since the very scientific criteria which made it implausible to claim human status for the pre-implantation embryo would establish a stronger claim for that status after implantation and individuation.

Authority and prudence

An argument of this kind, while approached in some of the Anglican and professional statements noted earlier in this chapter, is not apparent in official Roman Catholic statements. While holding no official position on the timing of ensoulment, the Roman Catholic Church at present interprets the wrongness of killing human beings as a principle which must be observed from conception or fertilisation. Therefore it might be suggested (in the light of the scientific evidence for making philosophical judgements) that this particular interpretation of a widely accepted general principle is largely dependent for its plausibility upon acceptance of the Roman Catholic Church's teaching authority. Again, the only other non-consequentialist argument for the particular interpretation is a prudential one against taking risks. As the 1974 Vatican statement puts it, 'the taking of life' after conception 'involves accepting the risk of killing a human being'.

Authority and prudence, then, would appear to be the major non-consequentialist arguments for the particular Roman Catholic interpretation of the two main moral ideas involved in the Churches' statements on AID, IVF and embryo research. Since no infallible statements are involved, authority appeals to teaching which, in principle, is capable of development and thus provides no ultimate safeguard against the kind of 'slippery slope' envisaged by the Catholic chaplain in the discussion. Nor perhaps does the appeal to prudence, since this, although one of the cardinal virtues, may neither be advanced above the others, nor reduced simply to caution.

'Slippery slope' or retrospective justification

In effect, it might be argued at this point, the particular moral interpretations enunciated by the Roman Catholic Church (and the other Churches insofar as they agree with it) offer protection against the 'slippery slope' only as long as the Churches (and Rome in particular) will them to do so. But in some quarters, it seems, this will may be weakening. Is this weakening in effect (as the Anglican chaplain suggested in the discussion) an opting for the 'teleological and utilitarian' retrospective justification of whatever technology dictates? This question, no doubt, raises a variety of large philosophical issues. However for the present purpose it might be suggested, briefly, that how it is to be answered may depend on one's view of human nature and the making of moral judgements.

Human nature and boundaries

The existence within the Churches of differing views of human nature was noted, for example, by the Anglican Social Responsibility Board in its Response to the Warnock Report. There was, the Board observed, a 'theological division ... concerning the extent to which nature is given by God with its ends determined, and the extent to which we may regard it as "raw material" to fashion for our own good ends'. The implication of the former view was that there were 'boundaries beyond which we should not transgress in altering the course of nature'.[10] This claim, of course, once again raises the question of how such boundaries are to be identified.

Products and submission

One possible way of deciding where 'to draw the line' is that proposed by the Catholic Committee on Bio-Ethical issues. The Committee argues that AID, IVF and even (if followed by selective abortion) antenatal diagnosis, are signs of the 'moral flaw' of regarding children as 'products' which 'typically are subject to quality control, utilisation and discard'. The proper alternative to this, the Committee argues, is 'a radical *submission*' by parents 'to the contingencies, however unforeseen' of their unreserved mutual commitment: parents, it continues, 'cannot rightly *determine* the character of their children or reject children whom they dislike'.[11] (A similar view, it may be recalled, was expressed by the school teacher in the discussion of abortion.)

'Making' as metaphor

In counselling 'submission' and warning against regarding children as 'products' this argument clearly deploys powerful metaphors against the illusion (as the *Choices in Childlessness* Report put it) 'that we can engineer for ourselves a problem-free and a pain-free utopia'.[12] In a 'technologically-minded' and 'consumer-oriented' society, this may seem a timely warning against transgressing natural boundaries. But how real in fact are the risks of this? The early eugenicists' dream of 'perfect children', surely, has now been discredited, not only by its Nazi perversion, but also by the realisation that imperfect and varied human beings are unlikely to agree on what shall constitute human perfection. In a totalitarian state, of course, the risks might be real. But the dangers to be avoided then, presumably, would be those of totalitarianism, rather than of the relatively modest and specific preventive advances of current (and foreseeable) reproductive and genetic medicine. Applied to these particular interventions of human artifice, moreover, the crude interpretation of 'making' a product seems inappropriate. The artist, after all, might be said to be engaged in 'making a product'. But this does not exclude the possibility of his work being done, lovingly, within the constraints of his medium, and to the end of creating something which properly may be regarded as 'having a life of its own'. The relationship even between artificer and artefact thus may be considerably less unequal than the metaphor at first suggests.

Submitting, determining and influencing

The notion of 'submission' also is problematic. In the past, after all, it was used in relation to many 'unforeseen contingencies' of marital commitment which health care, social welfare and family planning (including 'natural' family planning) have rendered avoidable. Moreover, in the immediate context of the argument, the notion that parents might '*determine* the character of their children' would seem no more desirable than it is possible. But again, perhaps, the argument may be missing the point. The alternative to 'submitting' to contingency may not be 'determining', but 'influencing' the character of children; and this is something which the Church, far from condemning, has commonly encouraged.

Genetic manipulation

In considering views of human nature which polarise the

142   *Life before birth*

discussion in terms of 'making' or 'submitting' and which regard nature as 'raw material' or 'given with its ends determined', the views of the Catholic theologian Karl Rahner may be noted. The choice of a marriage partner, Rahner pointed out, is only one of many 'methods of psychological, physiological and social self-manipulation' which human beings have long employed to the end of influencing the human future. The possibility that they might 'plan this manipulation rationally and steer it by means of technology', he argued, was not any different in principle.[13] The crucial ethical question was not whether or not to employ 'genetic manipulation', but whether a particular manipulation was 'appropriate to or contrary to the nature of man'.[14] Genetic manipulation in order to cultivate 'a species of intelligent animals which would live only unto themselves without being answerable for themselves',[15] would be an attempt to deny man's freedom and relation to the transcendent mystery of God; it thus would be immoral. Whether other genetic manipulations were 'appropriate to or contrary to the nature of man', Rahner suggested, could only be judged as the concrete possibility of each arose: they could not necessarily be ruled out in advance.

Human nature

Rahner's reasons for taking this view of genetic manipulation were based on what he believed to be 'a Christian understanding of nature'. According to this, 'man is not simply a product of "nature" as if nature *alone* were able and authorised to determine and model man's being'. On the contrary, 'man is characteristically the being who has been handed over to himself, consigned to his own free responsibility'.[16] Thus although man starts out 'from a "beginning", which is a prior datum and within a perspective of already pre-empted possibilities', human nature itself is such that man '*makes himself* what and who he wants to be and ultimately will be in the abiding validity and eternity of his free decisions'.[17]

Rahner's view thus suggests that human nature is best understood not as something fixed, but as a process of self-transcendence, effected through the exercise of responsible freedom and oriented to the goal of ultimate freedom in God. This view of human nature, it can be argued, is profoundly biblical in its orientation, in hope, to God and the future. It also takes account of the fact that human beings, lacking the more specific nature of other species, seem to have been left, as it were, 'unfinished'. It thus represents, in the contemporary world, what was described earlier as the more 'scientific' traditional Christian way of understanding the laws of nature.

On this view it might be argued that man 'submits' to his own nature precisely by his responsible 'making' of his own future; and that while human nature in one sense is 'given', it is not 'given with its ends determined' in any sense readily ascertainable without experiment. The crucial 'boundaries beyond which we should not transgress in altering the course of nature' are those whose crossing would entail renunciation of responsible freedom or of potential for humanity's ultimate goal. In this respect, therefore, human nature may be regarded 'as "raw material" to fashion for our own good ends', provided that those ends are determined in relation to human nature's self-transcending process and transcendent goal.

'Slippery slope' or process

This way of understanding human nature would seem to have significant implications for the discussion of a morally 'slippery slope' and the 'retrospective justification' of technological advance. If man has the freedom to make his own future, the 'Nuremberg' dangers envisaged by the 'slippery slope' metaphor clearly are among his options. But authority and caution may not be the sole safeguards against these dangers, and there may be a more rational alternative to 'the teleological and utilitarian justification of whatever technology dictates'. This alternative certainly would be teleological – it would be a matter, that is, of judging what technology proposed with reference to humanity's free, self-transcending process and its ultimate goal. But this teleological judgement could scarcely be called utilitarian (even in the widest sense of that word) since the ultimate transcendent 'utility' of the human process, by definition, 'passes man's understanding'.

Such teleological judgements then would not be a matter of justifying 'whatever technology dictates'. They thus offer a more rational and discriminating option than either fear of the 'slippery slope' or resigned 'retrospective justification'. However, as Rahner noted in the case of genetic manipulation, they do this at the cost of providing little or no moral guidance about technological advances which do not obviously entail renunci- ation of human freedom, responsibility and openness to the process of human self-transcendence. How moral questions about such advances are to be answered may, as suggested earlier, also depend upon one's view of the making of moral judgements.

Dominant moral arguments

A notable feature of many of the public statements recorded in this chapter is the extent to which moral judgements about AID, IVF, embryo research and other matters seem to have been made by focusing upon a particular kind of moral argument and allowing it to be the ultimate determining factor. The most obvious example of this is that while such bodies as the Medical Research Council or the Royal Society ultimately rely on consequentialist arguments, the Churches (and particularly the Roman Catholic Church) ultimately rely on deontological argu- ments about principles. The ways in which moral judgements are actually made are, of course, probably much more com- plicated than this.

As we have seen, consequentialist arguments are commonly used by the Churches to support deontological ones, and consideration of possible consequences may even be among the reasons why the Churches believe it important to take a stand on principle. Equally, scientific bodies advance consequentialist arguments in areas where the actual consequences, strictly speaking, are unknown; and this suggests that some principle (perhaps about the rightness of free scientific inquiry) may also be among their presuppositions.

Nevertheless, as the discussion also demonstrates, there seems to be a considerable divergence of opinion in this contemporary debate about which kind of moral argument should prevail. The difficulty with this divergence of opinion is that it seems to polarise moral debate in a way which excludes the possibility of public consensus as the basis for public policy on these import- ant questions.

The moral prism

But is such consensus possible? One way of opening up its possibility might be by questioning the need for moral judgements to be determined ultimately by the either-or of consequences versus principles. In a helpful metaphor, Professor Dorothy Emmett compares moral judgement to a prism:

> Ideally moral judgement might be a white light showing clearly what action would be best in any situation. But just as light coming through a prism is refracted into a spectrum of different colours, so our moral thinking shows us a range of different features, and attention can fasten now on one and now on another. And just as it is absurd to maintain that one colour in the spectrum is the only true, or even the truest form of light, so we must not make the mistake of assuming that one feature in the moral spectrum is the only true form of morality.[18]

What this metaphor might suggest in the present context is that neither consequentialist arguments nor deontological arguments, as different features in the moral spectrum, comprise 'the only true form of morality'. There is not, it is true, as Professor Emmett puts it, any 'satisfactory meta-ethical view which can harmonise the claims' of different kinds of moral argument 'under a unifying principle'. But in the case of conflicts between different kinds of argument, she suggests, 'the mediating factor is not an abstract principle but moral judgement, fallible yet capable of development, one condition of development being readiness to face this very complexity'.[19] The point here then is that, in making moral judgements, no particular kind of argument should be allowed a determining role in advance. The claims of each have to be considered in turn on their merits.

Conscience

But if the claims of different kinds of moral argument each have to be considered on their merits, by what and by whose criteria are these merits to be judged? In the case of moral judgement made by individuals, the classic Christian (both Catholic and Protestant) response is that the individual's conscience (the mind of man making moral judgements) itself is ultimately responsible before God for the moral judgements it makes. Part of this responsibility, of course, is for conscience to be as fully informed as possible, not only about what the Church teaches, but also about relevant factual matters, about moral factors such as those of intention, circumstances and consequences, and about different kinds of moral arguments with a bearing on the question addressed. Such is the complexity of all these factors however, that rational analysis of them may well not lead to *any* moral conclusion, let alone one about whose rightness one may be confident.

Moral wisdom

This difficulty is recognised by the Catholic theologian Karl Rahner, whose comments again seem pertinent. Discussing what it means to be a 'mature' or 'adult' Christian, Rahner suggests that

> there are times when no one can summon life's immensity of conditions and contingencies before the conventicle of conscience and so come to clear and free decisions. Much is simply done without testing and this is unavoidable. Hence none of us is completely mature and is to a large extent manipulated by biological and societal conditions.[20]

Nevertheless, Rahner argues, becoming mature or 'seasoned' in making moral judgements is a significant task to be undertaken; and part of maturity here is a synthesising of 'religiously dimensioned wisdom and moral instinct'.[21] Such moral wisdom, he writes elsewhere,

> can calmly take 'risks' provided that it is self-critically aware that its judgements contain unreflected elements which are, as such, contingent, subject to change and that consequently a *different* judgement may be shown to be correct at a later time. All the same, a particular contingent judgement of this kind can still be the only correct one *in its situation*.[22]

Interim judgements

Rahner's argument here is reminiscent of what is argued in at least one of the public statements noted earlier. The 1984

Council for Science and Society Working Party on *Human Procreation* states

> Moral judgements in so rapidly developing a field as this are at best interim judgements. It will be for our successors to revise them; and to work anew on questions as they arise. It would be arrogance, not social responsibility, to assume that if we have given no 'lead' on future possibilities, judgement will go by default. 'I am no better than my fathers'; and no wiser than my sons.[23]

A universal moral instinct

Having considered the spectrum of moral factors and arguments then, interim judgements may be the best we can hope for concerning many complex modern problems. This, however, does not entirely answer the question of the grounds on which such judgements are ultimately made. In this respect, an important aspect of Rahner's argument concerns what he called 'the universal moral instinct of faith and reason'. This 'moral knowledge', Rahner argues, 'has a structure which is both universal and not exhaustively analysable in conscious reflection'.[24] By means of this synthesising knowledge, the spectrum of morally relevant facts and arguments are 'correctly grasped in the "instinctive" judgement which recognises what is currently and properly called for, and this results in an "appropriate" judgement'. This claim, Rahner acknowledges, has its dangers ('especially when one thinks how much mischief and crime were perpetuated during the Nazi period in the name of "the healthy instinct of the people"'). Nevertheless, he argues, criticism of the possible dangers 'must neither dispute nor disregard the reality and rights of this universal instinct in reason and faith'.[25] This kind of moral knowledge has a particularly important role to play in many areas of modern life about which the Church has not made (and perhaps is not yet in a position to make) 'absolutely binding'[26] pronouncements.

Moral conflict as unavoidable

Through this 'moral faith-instinct' then, the Church and individuals may make appropriate and timely interim moral judgements about complex issues on which 'generally accepted norms ... lack the simple lucidity often attributed to them'.[27] One difficulty with this claim, however, is that the universality of this instinct may be disputed. Writing in the light of criticisms made of her Committee's Report, Lady Warnock has suggested that 'most ordinary people' would agree 'that moral distinctions, the basic distinctions between right and wrong, were drawn by moral sense and not by reason';[28] and that, alongside informed appraisal of all the facts and arguments, 'sentiment has some part, and indeed a crucial part, in arriving at moral decisions'. But the problem about this, she argues, is that'

> agreement is not always possible in matters of morality. We know that people's feelings differ. Therefore, moral conflict may be unavoidable. If morality were really a matter of weighing up harms and benefits, there would be more hope of agreement; and if it were a case of obeying certain rules, we ought to be able to find out what the rules lay down, and come to an agreed decision. In real life morality is more complicated and varied than that. There is no single 'correct' view.[29]

In the light of this conclusion, Lady Warnock has explained, the problem facing her Committee was that of what legislation to recommend when there seemed no possibility of moral agreement. British society was one in which '"common morality" is a myth'.[30] The moral problems which faced the Inquiry, moreoever, could not be left to 'moral experts'. 'Everyone's conscience is his own. The Protestant tradition founded on such belief runs very deep in this country.'[31]

Feelings and arguments

This conclusion, if accepted, would seem to rule out any appeal to 'universal' moral knowledge. It might even seem, in the end, to bring us back to what the surgeon in the discussion called 'gut feeling'. But in the discussion also, it may be remembered, the surgeon's claim was immediately questioned with reference to the arguments which preceded it; and the same arguments forced the gynaecologist to reconsider her contradictory pro-

fessional views about 'doing what the patient asks'. Without
drawing over-ambitious conclusions from these examples, the
least they suggest is (as Lady Warnock has also written) 'that a
decision is based on sentiment by no means entails that arguments cannot be adduced to support it'[32] – or to criticise it. It
may be possible, in other words, to refine sentiment by engaging
in rational moral discourse, in which the emotions may be
educated by learning more about relevant facts and arguments.

Polarisation in historical context

The difficulty with this suggestion is that, in practice, rational
moral argument does not seem to lead to moral consensus, or to
the recognition of some 'universal' moral knowledge in the light
of which interim judgements might be judged appropriate at a
particular time. Or at least it does not seem to do so *today*. One
reason for this, it might be suggested, is that the way in which
certain kinds of moral argument (deontological, consequentialist
and so forth) dominate the moral decision-making of different
bodies, is in fact a characteristic of a particular historical era.
This was caricatured, perhaps, by the doctor in the previous
chapter who contrasted 'pre-Reformation moral standards' with
'a post-Reformation moral debate'.

But it may not be entirely inaccurate to suggest that contemporary moral thinking has been skewed by polarisation such
as that between Catholic and Protestant, or religious and scientific,
or deontological and consequentialist ways of thinking; and
to suggest moreover that each of these ways of thinking
maintains its own position at least partly in reaction to the
other. One consequence of this would seem to be the need felt,
at one pole, to maintain particular traditional interpretations of
natural law and, at the other pole, to have nothing to do with
these 'metaphysical' considerations, and to conduct any argument
entirely in consequentialist terms.

Polarisation and mistrust

A negative concomitant of polarisation is the extent to which it
reflects mistrust between groups within society. The doctor who
spoke about 'pre-Reformation and post-Reformation' clearly

betrayed mistrust of the Churches' intentions; while on the other hand, Lady Warnock has remarked that society, despite its lack of a 'common morality', seems to have 'a corporate reaction' to the question of research using human embryos. 'It is', she writes, 'one of fear. People generally believe that science may be up to no good, and must not be allowed to proceed without scrutiny, both of its objectives and of its methods.'[33]

This judgement of popular sentiment may well be correct; and certainly there are neither historical nor theological grounds for assuming that scientists are any more exempt from original sin than anyone else. Therefore it is necessary, at the very least, for scientists to be prepared to explain and defend their work in public and for informed public interest to be represented in the control and direction of scientific advance. But insofar as these conditions are met, continuing mutual fear and suspicion seem an unpropitious environment for creative scientific work towards the public good. In particular, there appears something unsatisfactory in a historical situation in which two great moral enterprises of society – religion and science – regard one another with mistrust.

In this historical situation it may still seem unrealistic to suggest that ways of moderating this mistrust might be found. Nevertheless there may be some elements in the present moral debate which merit exploration to this end. The possible consequences of biomedical advance, for example, have often been discussed by many scientists and churchmen in a less than impartial spirit: but great benefits or great costs, prophesied in order to make political debating points, and then failing to materialise, do little to encourage confidence in either science or religion. Such political debates no doubt will continue; but alongside them there would seem to be some need for other more collaborative forms of inquiry, in which the issues are not prejudged before the scientific community, the Churches and other sections of society have had an opportunity to share both information and doubts.

Such forms of inquiry (in which at least some churchmen and scientists are already engaged) would be entirely within the spirit of the Christian natural-law tradition. One irony of the present historical situation, as the Reformed theologian J. M. Gustafson has observed, is that the natural-law tradition, 'intended to overcome serious disagreement on moral questions without recourse to historic particularities',[34] has become largely identified with a particular historical interpretation of its principles. Nevertheless, as was suggested earlier, the two natural-law principles discussed in this chapter, at least in their general form, may provide some basis for a wider consensus than is apparent at present.

The principle that 'the 'manner in which human faculties work indicates the ends which they are meant to serve, and also the means by which these ends might be attained' is one which, in these general terms, might seem right and reasonable to many people (provided that such faculties are not turned into ends in themselves). So too would the second principle, that it is wrong to kill innocent human beings. Exploration of the application and implications of these moral principles – for example, in the case of marriage and the family, or of embryos and foetuses – would necessarily involve rational inquiry, whose conclusions about the variety of natural ends and means would then have to be included in a reasoned public debate taking account of the different arguments in the moral spectrum. Having thus brought all these 'conditions and contingencies before the conventicle of conscience' (as Rahner puts it), conflicting sentiments might still prevent any agreement. On the other hand, it can fairly be said, an open discussion of this kind hitherto has largely been prevented by the fear and mistrust reflected in polarised positions. If this polarisation were moderated, the possibility of all the 'conditions and contingencies' being 'correctly grasped in the "instinctive" judgement of what is currently and properly called for' might emerge, and an 'appropriate' interim consensual judgement might be reached.

At present, clearly, this seems an unlikely possibility. If it is a possibility at all, however, it does raise for all those still defending their entrenched positions, including churchmen and scientists, the moral question of whether they would not be better to regard one another as critical friends, engaged in a common enterprise.

Notes

Introduction

1 G. Calabresi and P. Bobbit (1978), *Tragic Choices* (W. W. Norton, New York), p. 198.
2 ibid., p. 18.
3 J. Mahoney, SJ (1985), 'Moral reasoning in medical ethics' (*The Month*, Sept. 1985), p. 293.
4 ibid.
5 BCC and RC Liaison Committee (1978), *Public Statements on Moral Issues* British Council of Churches, London, and Catholic Information Services, Abbots Langley.
6 ibid., p. 8.
7 ibid., p. 11.
8 ibid., p. 9.
9 ibid.
10 ibid., p. 11.
11 ibid.
12 ibid., p. 13.
13 ibid., p. 14.
14 ibid.
15 ibid.
16 ibid., p. 21.
17 ibid.
18 ibid., p. 21f.
19 ibid.
20 ibid., p. 22.
21 ibid.
22 ibid., p. 23.
23 ibid.
24 ibid., p. 25.
25 I. E. Thompson (1979), *Dilemmas of Dying* and K. M. Boyd (1979), *The Ethics of Resource Allocation in Health Care*, The University Press, Edinburgh.

Chapter 1

1 *Abortion Act 1967*, ch. 87.
2 *R.* v. *Bourne* 1939.

3   *Abortion Act 1967.*
4   BMA (1984), *The Handbook of Medical Ethics* (BMA, London), p. 59.
5   ibid.
6   HMSO (1979), *A Bill To Amend the Abortion Act 1967* (Bill 7 50224), HMSO, London.
7   BMA (1984) p. 60.
8   J. K. Mason and R. A. McCall Smith (1983), *Law and Medical Ethics* (Butterworths, London), p. 58.
9   HMSO (1974), *Report of the Committee on the Working of the Abortion Act* Cmnd 5538, HMSO, London.
10 A. S. Duncan, G. R. Dunstan and R. B. Welbourn (2nd edn, 1981), *Dictionary of Medical Ethics* (Darton Longman and Todd, London), p. 132.
11 ibid., p. 136f.
12 The 35th World Medical Assembly, Venice, Italy, in October 1983 altered the phrase, 'from the time of conception,' to 'from its beginning'. BMA (1984), p. 70.
13 Duncan, Dunstan and Welbourn (1981), p. 137.
14 BMA (1984), p. 59.
15 See note 12 above.
16 BMA (1984), p. 59.
17 ibid.
18 General Medical Council (1983), *Professional Conduct and Discipline: Fitness to Practice* (GMC, London), p. 20.
19 Institute of Medical Ethics, *Bulletin No. 1*, April 1985, IME, London.
20 United Kingdom Central Council for Nursing, Midwifery and Health Visiting (1983), *Code of Professional Conduct*, UKCC, London.
21 CIO (1965), *Abortion: an Ethical Discussion* (Church Information Office, London), p. 31f.
22 CIS (1980), *Abortion and the Right to Live*, (Church Information Services, Abbots Langley), para. 6.
23 ibid., para. 7.
24 ibid., para. 11.
25 ibid., para. 12.
26 CIO (1965), p. 28.
27 ibid., p. 31.
28 ibid., p. 30.
29 ibid., p. 3.
30 CIO (1979), *General Synod, November 1979, Report of Proceedings*, vol. 10, no. 3 (CIO, London), p. 1158.
31 Church of Scotland (1966), *Reports to the General Assembly, Social and Moral Welfare Board* (Church of Scotland, Edinburgh), p. 475.

32 *Acta Apostolicae Sedis* (*AAS*) *Declaration on Abortion* (Issued by the Sacred Congregation for the Doctrine of the Faith, 18 November 1974), para. 1471.
33 ibid., para. 1472.
34 CIS (1980), para. 8.
35 ibid., para. 8.
36 CIO (1965), p. 33.
37 CIS (1980), para. 22f.
38 CIO (1965), p. 32.
39 *AAS* (1974), para. 1472.
40 ibid., para. 1474f.
41 CIS (1980), para. 14.
42 ibid., para. 16.
43 ibid., para. 29.
44 ibid., para. 18.
45 ibid., para. 19.
46 ibid., para. 20.
47 ibid., para. 21.
48 ibid., para. 22.
49 ibid., para. 23.
50 ibid., para. 24.
51 CIO (1965), p. 61.
52 Church of Scotland (1966), p. 475.
53 CIO (1965), p. 33.
54 ibid., p. 34
55 ibid., p. 36.
56 ibid., p. 61f.
57 ibid., p. 43.
58 ibid., p. 62.
59 Church Assembly (1966), *Report of Proceedings* 16 February 1966 (Church of England, London), p. 116.
60 SPCK (1967), *The Chronicle of Convocation* (Canterbury), 17 Jan. 1967 (SPCK, London), p. 6.
61 Church of Scotland (1966), pp. 473–6.
62 CIO (1965), p. 67.
63 G. R. Dunstan (1974), *The Artifice of Ethics* (SCM Press, London), p. 86f.
64 Church of Scotland (1967), *Reports to the General Assembly, Social and Moral Welfare Board* (Church of Scotland, Edinburgh), p. 511.
65 See e.g. General Synod (1975), *Abortion Law Reform* (GS 255); Church of Scotland (1975), *Reports to the General Assembly, Committee on Moral Welfare* (Church of Scotland, Edinburgh), pp. 331–5.
66 CIS (1980), para. 26.

Chapter 2

1   J. H. Newman (1872), *Fifteen Sermons Preached before the University of Oxford* (Rivingtons, London), p. 258f.

Chapter 3

1   Social scientists, for example, may ask what evidence there is for remarks such as those by the GP about girls being 'pretty inadequate in contraception', or women not being 'upset by terminations'. Historians may find comments about 'pre- and post-Reformation' simplistic and misleading. Moral philosophers and moral theologians may consider the discussion's use and contrast of terms such as 'utilitarian' and 'rights' lacking in both precision and subtlety.

2   BMA (1984), p. 59.

3   ibid., p. 77.

4   CIS (1980), para. 21.

5   G. Grisez (1972), *Abortion* (Corpus Books, New York), p. 182f.

6   W. M. Abbott SJ (1966). *The Documents of Vatican II* (Geoffrey Chapman, London/Dublin), p. 681.

7   CIS (1980), para. 24.

8   CIO (1965), p. 32.

9   ibid., p. 33.

10   In the case of *Roe* v. *Wade* (1973), the United States Supreme Court ruled that 'for the stage prior to approximately the end of the first trimester, the abortion decision and its effectuation must be left to the medical judgement of the pregnant woman's attending physician', This decision, in other words, effectively denied that the first trimester foetus had any legal rights in which the State had an interest. In arriving at this *legal* judgement, however, the Court noted the 'wide divergence of thinking' on *moral* judgements about this question. S. J. Reiser, A. J. Dyck and W. J. Curran (1977), *Ethics in Medicine* (MIT Press, London), pp. 401–15.

Chapter 4

1   HMSO (1960), *Report of the Departmental Committee on Artificial Human Insemination*, Cmnd 1105, HMSO, London.

2   DHSS (1984), *Report of the Committee of Inquiry into Human Fertilisation and Embryology*, Cmnd 9314 (HMSO, London), p. 19.

3   ibid.

4   CSS (1984), *Human Procreation: Ethical Aspects of the New Techniques* (OUP, Oxford), p. 14.

5   DHSS (1984), p. 23.
6   ibid., p. 9.
7   ibid., p. 10.
8   ibid., p. 11.
9   ibid., p. 12.
10 ibid., p. 15f.
11 ibid., p. 18.
12 ibid., p. 55.
13 ibid., p. 20.
14 ibid., p. 21.
15 ibid., p. 22.
16 ibid.
17 ibid., p. 23.
18 ibid., p. 27.
19 ibid., p. 25f.
20 ibid., p. 37.
21 ibid., p. 38.
22 ibid., p. 47.
23 ibid., p. 31.
24 ibid., p. 32.
25 ibid., p. 31.
26 ibid., p. 90f.
27 ibid., p. 32.
28 ibid., p. 75.
29 ibid., p. 77f.
30 ibid., p. 74.
31 ibid., p. 66.
32 ibid., p. 63.
33 ibid., p. 66.
34 ibid., p. 65.
35 ibid., p. 91.
36 ibid., p. 94.
37 ibid., p. 71f.
38 ibid., p. 55f.
39 ibid., p. 53f.
40 ibid., p. 56f.
41 DHSS (1972), *The Use of Fetuses and Fetal Material for Research*, HMSO, London.
42 DHSS (1984) op. cit., p. 64.
43 MRC (1985), *Report of Inquiry into Human Fertilisation and Embryology: Medical Research Council Response* (MRC, London), p. 5.
44 DHSS (1972), p. 5.
45 ibid., p. 8f.

46   ibid., p. 5f.
47   ibid., p. 7f.
48   MRC (1982), 'Research Related to Human Fertilisation and Embryology' (*British Medical Journal*, vol. 285, 20 Nov. 1982), p. 1480.
49   BMA (1983), 'Appendix VI: Interim Report on Human *In Vitro* Fertilisation and Embryo Replacement and Transfer' (*British Medical Journal*, vol. 286, 14 May 1983), p. 1594f.
50   RCOG (1983), *Report of the RCOG Ethics Committee on In Vitro Fertilisation and Embryo Replacement or Transfer*, Royal College of Obstetricians and Gynaecologists, London.
51   CSS (1984), op. cit.
52   Royal Society (1983), *Human Fertilisation and Embryology: Submission to DHSS Committee of Inquiry*, Royal Society, London.
53   RCGP (1983), 'Evidence to the Government Enquiry into Human Fertilisation and Embryology', Royal College of General Practitioners, London.
54   MRC (1985), op. cit.
55   MRC (1982), op. cit.
56   BMA (1983).
57   RCOG (1983), p. 14.
58   Royal Society (1983), p. 10f.
59   CSS (1984), p. 85.
60   ibid., p. 82.
61   MRC (1985), p. 4f.
62   RCOG (1983), p. 15f.
63   CSS (1984), p. 86.
64   MRC (1985), p. 5.
65   BMA (1983), op. cit.
66   RCOG (1983), p. 7f.
67   CSS (1984), p. 50f.
68   RCGP (1983), p. 2.
69   ibid., p. 1f.
70   RCGP (1983), Letter from the Honorary Secretary of Council, RCGP.
71   MRC (1985), p. 2f.
72   RCGP (1983), p. 1.
73   RCOG (1983), p. 13.
74   CSS (1984), p. 5f.
75   ibid., p. 52.
76   RCOG (1983), p. 13.
77   CSS (1984), p. 52.
78   RCOG (1983), p. 13f.
79   CSS (1984), p. 7.

80   CTS (1960), *Artificial Insemination: Evidence on Behalf of the Catholic Body in England and Wales* (Catholic Truth Society, London), p. 12.
81   ibid., p. 12f.
82   ibid., p. 13.
83   ibid., p. 6.
84   ibid., C. J. McFadden (1953), *Medical Ethics* (F. A. Davis, Philadelphia), p. 62.
85   ibid., p. 61.
86   ibid., p. 62.
87   CTS (1960), p. 14.
88   SPCK (1948), *Artificial Human Insemination* (SPCK, London), p. 58.
89   ibid., p. 56.
90   ibid., p. 54.
91   ibid., p. 61f.
92   ibid., p. 40.
93   ibid., p. 42.
94   ibid., p. 44.
95   ibid., p. 47.
96   ibid., p. 45f.
97   ibid., p. 51.
98   ibid., p. 50.
99   ibid., p. 62f.
100 CIO (1959), *Artificial Insemination by Donor: Two Contributions to a Christian Judgement* (Church Information Office, London), p. 21.
101 ibid., p. 16.
102 ibid., p. 22.
103 ibid., p. 19f.
104 ibid., p. 23.
105 CTS (1960), p. 3.
106 ibid., p. 4.
107 ibid., p. 4f.
108 ibid., p. 8ff.
109 ibid., p. 11f.
110 CIS (1983a), *Briefing: Catholics Women's Submission to the Warnock Committee*, Catholic Information Services, Abbots Langley.
111 CIS (1983b), *Briefing: Submission to the Government Enquiry into Human Fertilisation and Embryology from the Joint Ethico-Medical Committee of the Catholic Union of Great Britain and the Guild of Catholic Doctors*, Catholic Information Services, Abbots Langley.

112 CIS (1983c), *Human Fertilisation – Choices for the Future,* Catholic Information Services, Abbots Langley.
113 CIS (1983d), *In Vitro Fertilisation: Morality and Public Policy,* Catholic Information Services, Abbots Langley.
114 CMO (1985), *Response to the Warnock Report,* Catholic Media Office, London.
115 CIS (1983b), p. 3f.
116 CIS (1983c), p. 24.
117 CIS (1983a), p. 4.
118 CIS (1983c), p. 24.
119 CIS (1983d), p. 15.
120 CIS (1983a), p. 4; cf. CIS (1983b), p. 11.
121 CIS (1983c), p. 8.
122 ibid., p. 25f.
123 ibid., p. 27f.
124 ibid., p. 29ff.
125 CIS (1983b), p. 4.
126 CMO (1985), p. 9.
127 FCFC/BCC (1982), *Choices in Childlessness,* Free Church Federal Council/British Council of Churches, London.
128 ibid., p. 45.
129 ibid., p. 43.
130 ibid., p. 45.
131 ibid., p. 44.
132 ibid., p. 54.
133 ibid., p. 52.
134 Church of Scotland (1985), *Reports to the General Assembly, Board of Social Responsibility* (Church of Scotland, Edinburgh), p. 290.
135 Church of England (1984), *Human Fertilisation and Embryology* (Board for Social Responsibility, London), p. 9ff.
136 SPCK (1948), p. 9.
137 CIO (1959), p. 22.
138 FCFC/BCC (1982), p. 21.
139 Church of Scotland (1985), p. 290.
140 CIS (1983d), p. 6.
141 ibid., p. 7.
142 CIS (1983c), p. 20.
143 CIS (1983d), p. 8f.
144 CIS (1983c), p. 21.
145 ibid.
146 CIS (1983d), p. 10.
147 CIS (1983a), p. 4.
148 CIS (1983b), p. 4.

149   CIS (1983d), p. 14.
150   ibid., p. 16.
151   ibid., p. 12.
152   CMO (1985), p. 3.
153   ibid., p. 6.
154   ibid., p. 5.
155   ibid., p. 13.
156   ibid., p. 8f.
157   CIS (1983d), p. 10f.
158   FCFC/BCC (1982), p. 36.
159   ibid., p. 42f.
160   ibid., p. 54.
161   ibid., p. 46.
162   ibid., p. 55.
163   ibid., p. 47.
164   ibid., p. 48.
165   ibid., p. 55.
166   Church of England (1984), p. 15f.
167   Church of Scotland (1985), p. 291.
168   Church of England (1984), p. 14.
169   Church of England (1984), p. 13f.
170   ibid., p. 13.
171   ibid., p. 7f.
172   ibid., p. 16f.
173   Church of England (1985), *Personal Origins*, Board for Social Responsibility, London. See also: Church of England, *General Synod Report*, Feb. 1985, vol. 15, no. 1 (Church Information Office, London), p. 7f.; Institute of Medical Ethics, *Bulletin No. 4*, July 1985 (IME, London), p. 7.
174   Church of Scotland (1985), p. 288.
175   ibid., p. 290f.
176   ibid., p. 289.
177   Church of Scotland (1984), *Reports to the General Assembly, Board of Social Responsibility* (Church of Scotland, Edinburgh), p. 360.
178   Church of Scotland (1975), *Reports to the General Assembly, Committee on Moral Welfare* (Church of Scotland, Edinburgh), p. 328.
179   Church of Scotland (1973), *Reports to the General Assembly, Committee on Church and Nation* (Church of Scotland, Edinburgh), p. 53.
180   Church of Scotland (1985), *Reports to the General Assembly, Board of Social Responsibility* (Church of Scotland, Edinburgh), p. 287.

181 W. Paul (1985), 'Challenge to Kirk Stance on Abortion', (*The Scotsman*, 20 May, 1985), p. 7, col. 8.
182 Church of Scotland (1986), *The Gist: Assembly Summary 1986* (Church of Scotland, Edinburgh).

Chapter 6

1 Not least questionable are those which the GP seems to have sought as his quarry in stalking the gynaecologist. What is suggested about the values of working-class IVF candidates may have been sufficiently questioned in the discussion itself. But the GP's attempt to attribute tubal obstruction to sexually transmitted disease, although not entirely successful, is more serious because a similar suggestion was subsequently made by the Catholic Committee on Bio-Ethical issues in its Response to the Warnock Report. Unfortunately the Catholic Committee cited no authority for this suggestion, and (in the absence of published research) information subsequently sought for the present purpose from an infertility clinic stated that tubal blockage commonly seemed to be caused by infections following pregnancy and birth; the proportion of cases in which it followed abortion or use of the IUD (along with sexually transmitted diseases, the main causes alleged by the Catholic Committee) was much smaller.
2 Institute of Medical Ethics (1985), *Bulletin No. 1* (IME, London), p. 3.
3 CTS (1980), p. 3.
4 SPCK (1948), p. 62.
5 CTS (1980), p. 3.
6 SPCK (1948), p. 50.
7 CIS (1983c), p. 8.
8 SPCK (1948), p. 63.
9 See J. Mahoney SJ (1984), *Bioethics and Belief* (Sheed and Ward, London), ch. 3; G. R. Dunstan (1984), 'The Moral Status of the Human Embryo: a Tradition Recalled' (*Journal of Medical Ethics*, 1984, 1), pp. 38–44.
10 Church of England (1984), p. 14.
11 CIS (1983d), p. 15f.
12 FCFC/BCC (1982), p. 42.
13 K. Rahner SJ (1972), *Theological Investigations IX* (Darton Longman and Todd, London), p. 228.
14 ibid., p. 230.
15 ibid., p. 231.
16 ibid., p. 227.
17 ibid., p. 228.

18 D. Emmett (1979), *The Moral Prism* (Macmillan, London), p. 1.
19 ibid., p. 147.
20 K. Rahner sj (1984), 'Reflections on the Adult Christian', (*Theology Digest*, 31:2, Summer 1984), p. 123.
21 ibid., p. 124.
22 Rahner (1972), p. 239.
23 CSS (1984), p. 7.
24 Rahner (1972), p. 238.
25 ibid., p. 239.
26 Rahner (1984), p. 125.
27 ibid., p. 124.
28 M. Warnock (1985), *A Question of Life* (Basil Blackwell, Oxford), p. viii.
29 ibid., p. x.
30 ibid., p. xi.
31 ibid., p. 96.
32 ibid., p. x.
33 ibid., p. xiii.
34 J. M. Gustafson (1981), *Theology and Ethics* (Basil Blackwell, Oxford), p. 79.

Index